T0156518

Designing Planned Communities
Communities

Designing Planned Communities

Daniel R. Mandelker

iUniverse, Inc.
New York   Bloomington

Designing Planned Communities

Copyright © 2010 Daniel R. Mandelker

All rights reserved. No part of this book may be used or reproduced by any means, graphic, electronic, or mechanical, including photocopying, recording, taping or by any information storage retrieval system without the written permission of the publisher except in the case of brief quotations embodied in critical articles and reviews.

Cover Art:
The Perry Neighborhood
Lane Kendig, Strategic Advisor, Kendig Keast Collaborative

Back Cover Photo:
Washington University
Mary Butkus

iUniverse books may be ordered through booksellers or by contacting:

iUniverse
1663 Liberty Drive
Bloomington, IN 47403
www.iuniverse.com
1-800-Authors (1-800-288-4677)

Because of the dynamic nature of the Internet, any Web addresses or links contained in this book may have changed since publication and may no longer be valid. The views expressed in this work are solely those of the author and do not necessarily reflect the views of the publisher, and the publisher hereby disclaims any responsibility for them.

ISBN: 978-1-4502-0923-6 (pbk)
ISBN: 978-1-4502-0925-0 (cloth)
ISBN: 978-1-4502-0924-3 (ebook)

Printed in the United States of America

iUniverse rev. date: 03-08-10

For Daniel
Forever Blessed

Contents

List of Featured Articles

List of Images, Photos, and Maps

Preface and Acknowledgments

When I completed my Planning Advisory Service Report on *Planned Unit Developments* for the American Planning Association, I was struck by the need for more discussion of urban design issues in planned communities. I then decided it might be useful to do a follow-up study on this topic. That was the starting point for this book.

I expected to find design principles for the design of planned communities, make suggestions on how to incorporate them into planned community ordinances, and deal with what I thought was a difficult line of court decisions. I did not find what I expected. Contemporary design principles are available for mixed-use and retail town and village centers. Neighborhood design still follows principles developed years ago, though there are modern variations, as in New Urbanist traditional neighborhood development. There seems to be a consensus among design principles at the site, building, and streetscape level. Commentary on design principles for the design of planned community projects was disappointing, however, though case studies are plentiful.

Translating design principles into design standards for planned community ordinances proved more difficult than expected. Providing general statements of basic design themes or a generally stated design principle is possible, but specifying planned community design can take pages of explanation that do not fit well into zoning ordinances for planned communities. Providing these standards is possible, however, and chapter four contains a number of examples. One alternative is to provide a set of design indicators (rather than design standards) in the ordinance that can provide guidance for the design process. I also learned that local governments often turn to comprehensive plans, guidelines, and manuals to find design standards, which is why I have included a separate chapter about these design documents.

Another concern I had as I began this project was that a group of hostile court decisions had held design standards unconstitutionally vague, which seemed to make their inclusion in planned community ordinances difficult. My research found that the cases were more favorable than I expected. There are not that many court decisions, but some of the hostile cases are from states that take strict views on constitutional issues such as vagueness and delegation of power. When design standards are part of a comprehensive ordinance for a planned community, they have a much better chance of surviving legal attack.

The format and approach of this book, then, requires explanation. It is similar to the format and approach I used in my report entitled *Planned Unit Developments*. It is not a critique of design theory for planned communities. It does not propose design solutions for these communities. Rather, it summarizes existing principles about planned community design and translates them into design standards. I do not have a point of view on what kind of design is good or preferable in a planned community. My goal is simply to show how design principles that are available can be made workable by local governments.

The first chapter discusses the design review problem in planned communities, and outlines what I call a "design framework" that must be taken into account in the design of planned communities. This design framework includes project elements such as landscaping, circulation systems, streetscapes, and parking. The design process for planned communities may consider some of these design frameworks, but decisions on them often lie outside the design process and are based on separate and independent requirements. Parking standards are an example.

Chapter two reviews design principles and practice for the design of planned communities and for the design of different project elements in these communities such as town centers and neighborhoods. You can call this chapter a literature review. Chapter three discusses and gives examples of design standards in comprehensive plans, guidelines, and manuals, while chapter four discusses and gives examples of design standards in planned community ordinances. Chapter five discusses the legal issues raised by design standards.

Some comment is necessary on why the book is organized as it is. I could have divided the text into separate chapters on each of the design issues that planned communities present. One chapter, for example, could have considered design issues at the project level, and then discuss how design standards have been developed for these issues in all possible formats. Other chapters could have considered each of the project elements in planned communities.

I decided, however, that the format in which a design issue is placed has an important effect on how it should be discussed. Design standards in manuals, for example, present different issues than design standards in ordinances. This concern explains the chapter organization. There is some overlap as a result. Design principles for town centers, for example, are discussed in chapter two, while examples of how these principles are applied are included in the next two chapters. Chapter four uses some examples of guidelines from chapter three in its discussion of design standards in planned community ordinances.

I hope this overlap will enrich rather than confuse. I have included cross-references to help the reader.

I have provided Internet addresses for plans, documents, and other materials. Some quotations from these documents are included in the book, and the Internet can provide access to the full text. These addresses may change as local governments, especially, often move documents to new locations. But the material may usually be found on the government's Web site. I also expect to post the images in the book on my Web site, law.wustl.edu/landuselaw.

I would like to thank the many people who assisted me in writing this book. All or parts of the book were reviewed by Uri Arvin, Lane Kendig, Robert J. Little, Wayne Mortensen, Darcie White, my daughter Amy, and anonymous reviewers, all of whom made helpful suggestions. Telephone, personal, and e-mail interviews with Frank Bangs, Jonathan Barnett, Tim Busse, Tim Curtis, Bob Einsweiler, Lee D. Einsweiler, Albert Elias, Catherine Fabacher, Ajay Garde, Susan Istenes, Lane Kendig, Matthew Lewis, Robert J. Little, Mathhew Lewis, Jim Mazzocco, Joe McHarris, Gary Oldehehoff, Paul Sedway, Darcie White, and Nore Winter were very helpful. Andrea Donze, my assistant, and Beverly Owens, Assistant Director for Faculty Support, offered invaluable assistance, as did Kathie Molyneaux and other members of our library staff. Darcie White, Lane Kendig, and my research assistant Lauren Smith graciously contributed featured articles. I especially would also like to thank Bob Jacob, Carey Hayo, Lane Kendig, Gary Vogrin, Darcie White, and Micah Wood for contributing their graphic images. I am especially grateful to Kent Syverud, dean of our law school, for the research support that made this book possible. Many thanks to all. Of course, I am responsible for all of the statements and ideas contained in my book.

Daniel R. Mandelker
Stamper Professor of Law
Washington University in St. Louis
January 14, 2010

Chapter One
The Design Problem in Planned Communities

Planned communities are a dominant form of development, both in suburban areas and as infill in urban settings. Planned communities can be clusters of homes with common open space or master-planned communities covering thousands of acres, but in any form they provide opportunities for excellent design. This book reviews the concepts and ideas that go into the design of planned communities, and explores how local governments can encourage and provide for their good design through land-use regulation.

WHAT PLANNED COMMUNITIES ARE AND WHY WE HAVE THEM

The compositional form of most planned communities defines their development structure. They became popular because of development problems that arose under traditional zoning and subdivision regulations, which did not originally include this concept. The zoning ordinance regulates land uses and lot sizes. The subdivision ordinance regulates street and block layouts and requires developers to provide public infrastructure such as streets, sewers, and other utilities. There is a gap here. Neither ordinance gives designers or developers the flexibility to design a planned community that includes common open space, resource protection, and better and varied design. Worse, these ordinances penalize the developer who seeks to provide open space or to preserve natural resource areas.

Zoning and subdivision regulations provided adequate control so long as development occurred at fairly high densities, one block at a time, in the grid pattern then typical of cities. This pattern determined the design of new development. Public agencies provided open space. This pattern changed when large-scale developers began to appear early in the twentieth century who prepared master plans for the early streetcar suburbs. Development patterns changed even more dramatically after the Second World War as individual builders of single homes gave way to large-scale builders who built large projects planned as an entity, often with hundreds of dwellings. Zoning and subdivision ordinances in place at the time were insufficient and could not be used to review the design and character of these new, large-scale developments.

Variety in design was not possible because statutes required uses to be uniform within zoning districts. This meant that lot sizes and site requirements had to be uniform for each development project because each was located in a single zoning district. Mixed-use developments were not possible unless different zoning was established for each section of a development, which is impracticable. Developers then adopted economic models for their developments that required building to minimum zoning and subdivision standards and provided residential projects with uniform lot sizes and site features. This approach created a monotonous style called "cookie-cutter development" in popular criticism. Planned communities appeared as an alternative that would allow local governments to achieve objectives they could not achieve under traditional land-use regulation, such as better and more varied design, though these terms, being subjective, are difficult to define. Form-based zoning codes and other innovations such as conservation subdivisions have also helped to modernize traditional zoning and subdivision controls, but they do not allow for the flexibility in the design of development projects that is possible under planned community regulations.

It will help to have a definition of a planned community:

A planned community is a development that has been approved through a comprehensive review of projects characterized by an integrated and unified design. It may include a variety of project types including infill developments, housing developments, mixed-use developments, and master-planned communities.

This definition describes a planned community both as a type of development and a process. It defines a process because it includes any type of development that cannot be built under conventional zoning and subdivision regulations, and which therefore requires a comprehensive review that results

Components of a Planned Community

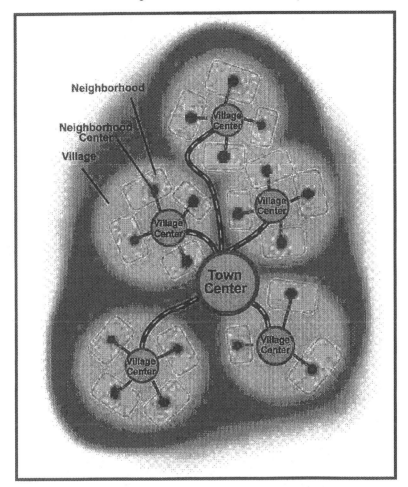

Planned Community Components
Houghton Area Master Plan, Tucson, Arizona

in the approval of a development plan. The definition also covers a variety of development types as planned communities. Three types of planned communities can be identified for purposes of considering design issues:

- **Cluster housing or cluster development**. These projects are single-family residential developments whose principal characteristic is that housing is clustered in one area of the project in return for the provision of common open space in areas not taken by housing. Density is higher in the area of the project where housing is clustered, but there is no overall increase in density. The principal problem is the tradeoff between the clustering of residential units in the clustered area and the provision of common open space as a compensatory feature. These projects are usually limited in size. Design issues can arise when deciding on the design of the project as a residential neighborhood and on the design of sites and buildings.

- **Mixed-use developments**. These projects combine residential and nonresidential uses such as commercial and office uses. They often include multistory buildings and may attempt to achieve a main street character. They are usually of moderate size and are often built as infill developments in urban areas. Planned community villages that are recommended for rural areas are another example of a mixed-use development that may incorporate a village center with retail and office uses. Issues can arise in deciding on the design of a mixed-use development, the character of a village center, and the design of residential neighborhoods and their housing.

- **Master-Planned Communities.** A master-planned community is a planned community, usually on substantial acreage, that combines employment, office, retail, and entertainment centers, often mixed in use, with associated self-contained neighborhoods. A master-planned community can be a new town. Often, these communities are required to have a minimum size of between 600 and 1,000 acres. Their size and scale require a phased planning and development process. These communities raise complex design issues at the project level for the various types of centers within the project, and for residential neighborhoods and their housing.

"Planned unit development" has historically been the term used to describe all of the planned community types discussed here, and is the term most commonly used in statutes and ordinances. It is a bit archaic today, however, and this book uses the term "planned community" to describe any type of development that is comprehensively planned and developed as an entity with a single development vision. It may be built by a single developer or multiple developers. I use the term "planned unit development" only when ordinances and documents discussed in the text use this term.

THE DESIGN FOCUS

This book focuses to a great extent on the design problems raised by larger master-planned communities, including the overall design of the planned community along with the design of town and village centers and residential

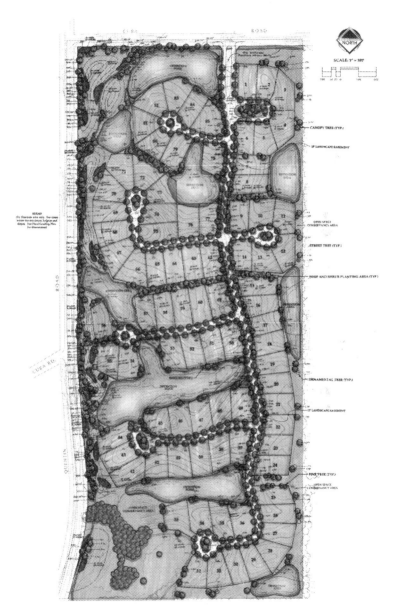

Ponds of Kildeer, Kildeer, Illinois
Lane Kendig, Strategic Advisor
Kendig Keast Collaborative

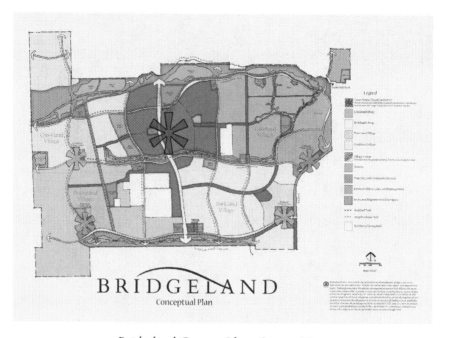

Bridgeland Concept Plan, Cypress, Texas
Carey S. Hayo, AICP, Principal, and Blake Drury, AICP, Senior
Program Designer
Glatting Jackson Kercher Anglin, Inc.

neighborhoods within these communities. Design standards for town centers and neighborhoods are also needed, however, in more limited planned communities. For example, design issues for residential neighborhoods and town centers must be addressed in mixed-use planned communities. Site and building design issues are present in all planned communities.

Cluster housing projects present somewhat different design issues because they are residential neighborhoods with a common open space feature, and it is difficult to think of them as "planned" communities. Nevertheless, cluster housing presents the same design issues as larger planned communities at the neighborhood and housing level. Some examples in this book are specifically based on cluster housing communities. The term "cluster housing" is used when this type of development is discussed.

DEFINING DESIGN STANDARDS FOR PLANNED COMMUNITIES

At the outset, it should be recognized that design standards for planned communities present different regulatory and legal issues than the regulations created by zoning ordinances. The zoning ordinance establishes districts in which land uses are allowed as a matter of right. A planned community ordinance can also define the type of planned community that is allowed as of right, but this is not typical. Instead, the planned community ordinance usually establishes a discretionary review process that ends with the approval of a development plan for the planned community. Design standards can be included in the standards for the approval of a planned community, and the reviewing body will then consider design along with other standards when deciding whether to approve a planned community. These review and decision-making processes are vastly different from the establishment of zoning districts with as-of-right uses. The planned community ordinance requires the adoption of design standards that can produce the kind of design that is expected.

In its use of approval standards to guide decisions on project acceptability, the planned community ordinance resembles the subdivision control ordinance, which also contains standards that the reviewing body must apply in a discretionary review process that can result in the approval of a subdivision. The difference is that most approval standards in subdivision control ordinances are quantitative and require little or no discretion in their application. Standards for the width and paving of streets are an example. Design review standards for planned communities can be quantitative as well; for example, a standard may limit the length of building facades. Qualitative standards can also be included that require an exercise of judgment in their application. An illustrative, but not necessarily good, example is a design standard that requires "innovative design" in planned communities. Defining and developing good design standards for planned communities is a critical and somewhat difficult task.

Design standards cannot be adopted without a definition of what good design is. It is widely recognized that the depth of the term *design* makes its definition ambiguous. The word has many dimensions that cannot precisely be described. Deciding on what design means and what its scope should be is a critical issue. A decision must be made on whether design review should focus only on the visual qualities of the urban environment or, more broadly, on the organization and management of urban space (Carmona et al. 2003, 3).

Resolving ambiguities associated with the scope of design review is an important task. A narrow view of design would focus only on individual buildings and the design of neighborhoods. A narrow view would also focus only on appearance, such as the appearance of buildings, and not on the organization and management of space within a project. Translated, a narrow view would require only an appearance code in planned community regulations that would regulate the appearance of buildings and structures. A broad view of design would go further and include the organization and management of urban space. It would require design standards for the planned community and for each level in the development. This book takes both views. It examines the visual aspect of design as applied to planned communities, and the organization and management of space within these communities.

The scale at which design review is applied varies, with review for small-scale developments differing greatly from review for large-scale developments. At the smaller scale, the focus is on site design, impact on adjoining developments, connectivity, and combining many small developments over time to create a neighborhood. Cluster housing is an example. Design issues focus on residential forms.

For large-scale planned communities, the designer has control over an area sufficient to create an entire new town. Design must address large-scale infrastructure issues, and must focus on creating a community that works internally. Design must also address different levels in the planned community at different scales, beginning with the project as a whole and proceeding down through town center, village, and neighborhood. An important initial decision, though one seldom addressed, should be made at the regional level. Here, a planning framework should be established that integrates planned community planning policies with regional planning policies. A framework plan at this level can prevent the development of planned communities that are isolated, built at the wrong location or at the wrong scale, or that will not be served by adequate public services and facilities.

Similar planning issues arise for mixed-use planned communities, though on a lesser scale. A planning policy for these communities should be included in local comprehensive plans that can address density and public facility and service issues that are raised by these projects. Cluster housing does not create changes in density levels or service requirements, but plans should contain policies for the integration of these developments with adjacent neighborhoods and open space systems.

How Design Standards Should be Used

Deciding on an approach to design standards for planned communities raises a number of issues. A preliminary issue is whether a standard should provide incentives for better design or whether it should be regulatory. An

Pasadena Hills, Pasco County, Florida: How to Connect to Everything
Carey S. Hayo, AICP, Principal, and Blake Drury, AICP, Senior Program
Designer
Glatting Jackson Kercher Anglin, Inc.

incentive design standard would offer a benefit for better design, usually as an increase in density. This approach is often used in cluster housing regulations. This discussion focuses, however, on regulatory design standards that must be satisfied as a condition for the approval of a planned community.

There are several approaches to the approval process that ensures that planned communities are in compliance with design standards. It can be an administrative process conducted by staff or the planning commission. Or, it can be a legislative process conducted by the legislative body with a preliminary review by the planning commission. There should be a strong public review process that invites public participation through high visibility.

Though discretionary review processes may vary, each is completed with the approval of a development plan in text and graphics that contains the guidelines for the planned community, including requirements for uses, densities and intensities, circulation systems, and open space. The development plan can specify the design of the planned community and may include drawings and digital renderings to indicate design features.

Design elements in the plans for planned community development are based on and reflect design standards contained in a comprehensive plan, design guidelines, or manuals, or regulations in the planned community ordinance.

9

Design standards in these documents can be indeterminate or fixed. An indeterminate standard is a qualitative standard that specifies design objectives in qualitative terms such as *creative* or *innovative*. A fixed design standard is quantitative and contains an absolute rule. An example is a requirement that no more than 50 percent of a building facade may be a blank wall.

The standards that are adopted are interrelated with the type of process that is used. Ideally, there should be either a limited number of indeterminate standards counterbalanced by a strong and publicly visible review process that can add specificity, or fixed design standards with mostly administrative approvals on the assumption that the fixed standards protect the public interest. The first alternative is appropriate for larger projects where flexibility in providing design opportunities is important, while the second alternative can be used for more limited projects, such as cluster housing. Neither alternative is without problems. Indeterminate standards can lead to arbitrary decision making and present constitutional problems, while fixed standards can be too rigid. Many planned community regulations are hybrids that contain both types of standards.

If indeterminate qualitative standards are considered, the next question is to decide whether to adopt prescriptive standards that specify particular design objectives or design objectives that can guide a design process in which developers and designers have the freedom to create their own design solutions. The interest in prescriptive standards is driven in part by the assumption, implicit in the planned community approach to development, that planned communities will be better designed than traditional developments, but require prescriptive standards to ensure that this objective will be achieved. Here is one attempt at defining the design that is required for a planned community:

> [Planned community] architecture should demonstrate the cohesive planning of the development and present a clearly identifiable design feature throughout. It is not intended that buildings should be totally uniform in appearance, or that designers and developers should be restricted in their creativity. Rather, cohesion and identity can be demonstrated in similar building scale or mass; consistent use of facade materials; similar ground-level detailing, color or signage; consistency in functional systems, such as roadway or pedestrian way surfaces, signage, or landscaping; the framing of outdoor open space and linkages, or a clear conveyance in the importance of various buildings and features on the site (Somerville, Massachusetts 1990, § 16.7).

Cohesion and identity appear to be the key design elements required by this ordinance. The ordinance also gives examples of how these objectives can be attained, and sets forth elements of the project that must be considered in a design program.

The design-process method requires the inclusion of design objectives that guide this process and identify the design issues that reviewers should be considering. The reviewing body then decides whether the design objectives have been adequately considered. In natural resource protection, for example, reviewers may be directed to look not only at the resources being protected, but at protective measures that maximize habitat, water quality, or other objectives. The idea is to focus the review.

A design manual prepared for the then English Department of the Environment, Transport and Regions in London illustrates the range of design objectives that can guide the design process approach (Commission for Architecture & the Built Environment 2000, 15, 16). The manual lists seven design objectives that can apply to the design of planned communities:

- Character, a place with its own identity
- Continuity and Enclosure, a place where public and private places are clearly distinguished
- Quality of the Public Realm, a place with attractive and successful outdoor areas
- Ease of movement, a place that is easy to get through
- Legibility, a place that has a clear image and is easy to understand
- Adaptability, a place that can change easily
- Diversity, a place with variety and choice

Other design objectives can be included, and this list omits natural resource area preservation, but it illustrates the type of design objectives that can be adopted for the design process. Some of the objectives may need supplementation and explanation: character, for example, should not be confused with marketing or branding, and ease of movement should not be limited to an emphasis on vehicular traffic.

One of these indicators—legibility—was given prominence in an early influential book by Kevin Lynch, *The Image of the City* (Lynch 1960), though Lynch later modified his concepts (Lynch 1981, 118). Planners for the Irvine Ranch planned community in California were influenced by Lynch's legibility concept, which includes elements of edges, paths, districts, and landmarks (Forsyth 2005, 73-4).

A second set of indicators in the department's design manual covers aspects of development form such as layout, landscape, density and mix, height and massing, and appearance. They allow choice. The layout for urban grain, for example, allows a choice between "the degree to which an area's lots and plot subdivisions are respectively small and frequent (small grain), or large and infrequent (coarse grain)" (Id., 16).

Another example of design standards as performance indicators is the "Original Ahwahnee Principles" drafted in 1991 by a group that included leaders of the New Urbanism urban design movement (California Local Government Commission 1991). This document defines a community as a place where housing and other needs are located within walking distance of each other. It calls for street connectivity and an end to monotonous, look-alike buildings. Development must be compact, and public open space must be framed with buildings that open onto it. Resource-efficient land-use planning should preserve natural resources. Regional principles call for planning to be integrated around a transit network. Implementation principles call for the updating of plans to include the Ahwhanee Principles following an open process, and the adoption of a specific or precise plan as the basis for project development. The Ahwanee Principles have received substantial acceptance as a basis for the development of planned communities.

MARKETING DECISIONS AND PRODUCT MIX

Market decisions have a major influence on design standards for planned communities, as these communities are built for particular markets. If the planned community is a golf course community, that project objective will influence project design. If it is an affordable housing community, that project objective will influence project design. Marketing decisions also determine project size. Larger projects require complex design decisions on the structure and design of the project and its centers and neighborhoods. They also require greater flexibility so that they can adjust to market conditions over a decade or more. These issues are less complex in smaller projects. Product mix is another major issue. A cluster housing development with residential homes and common open space requires one kind of design. A master-planned community with a variety of housing and mixed uses requires a variety of designs. These are obvious points that need emphasis.

DESIGN FRAMEWORKS FOR PLANNED COMMUNITIES

The broad definition of design adopted here includes a wide variety of project elements. Some of these project elements make up one part of the built environment, which is the mass of buildings and structures in the planned community and the way in which they are organized. The design standards discussed in this book apply to these project elements. Another set of project elements, landscaping and circulation systems for example, make up another part of the built environment and provide design frameworks that influence and provide a framework for the design of a planned community.

Decisions about the project elements that make up the design frameworks may be made in the design process for a planned community, but they may also be made outside that process and may not be considered design issues. In addition, there is often an independent body of principles and standards that applies to design frameworks and that must be observed in addition to any design standards that may apply to planned communities. These design frameworks are discussed next.

Natural Resource Preservation Areas and Common Open Space

The natural topography and the environment in which a planned community is built have a major influence on its design, and natural resource preservation and design is a major design framework in any planned community. Planned communities can also be built in topographically demanding and definitive locations such as mountain tops, where topography is a major design influence. Other planned communities may be built in similarly distinctive natural environments such as a desert environment or a hilly terrain. Special regulations may apply in some of these environments; for example, regulations that limit development on steep slopes in hilly areas. These regulations can limit project density, require special design treatments, and include specially tailored landscaping and road design requirements. (Olshansky 1996). Wetlands and floodplain areas, such as federally designated floodplains, are another example. Performance zoning codes can also include specific levels of protection for all resources.

Planned community regulations can address natural resource preservation by requiring more resource preservation than other laws require or by including specific design standards for specific resources. Public ownership or enforceable property restrictions may be required. The trend is toward more, not less, preservation of natural resource areas, and 40 percent of preservation requirements have appeared in some planned community regulations. Extensive preservation at this level may pressure developers to increase density or encourage clustering, which will have an effect on project design.

Requirements for the provision of recreational common open space also remain typical in planned community regulations. It is especially important in cluster housing, where the provision of common open space is a trade-off for higher densities in some parts of the development. Planned community regulations can include requirements that define the location and accessibility of common open space, and its character and function, though the regulations may reflect standards that have been adopted for open space and recreational areas wherever they are located. Open space requirements influence the design of a planned community, and integrating the location and character of common open space with housing and other developed areas presents an important design challenge. Some commentators have referred to the network of open and recreational spaces as the landscape framework for a planned community (Forsyth 2005, 225). The network has also been called the "green infrastructure" framework.

Carrying Capacity Studies

Concerns about the preservation of natural resource areas in planned communities are sometimes met through a planning technique known as a carrying capacity study. This type of study gained prominence through an early and now classic book by the landscape architect Ian McHarg, *Design with Nature*. The planning process McHarg advocates assigns values to natural and human resources that pose limitations on development. A map is prepared for each resource, and a composite is then prepared whose cumulative set of values shows areas where development cannot occur or must be limited (McHarg 1969). In some planned communities, critical carrying capacity issues such as water management have provided a major basis on which development is structured.

An American Planning Association report describes in more detail how carrying capacity analysis is done:

> [Carrying capacity] analysis is an assessment of the ability of a natural system to absorb population growth as well as other physical development without significant degradation. Understanding the carrying capacity or constraints of natural resources (particularly ground and surface water systems) provides local governments with an effective method for identifying which portions of the community or region are most suitable sites for new and expanded development. Similarly, knowledge of carrying capacity limitations allows local government residents and officials to make more rational and defensible decisions regarding how and where development may occur (Meck 2002, 7–176).

Carrying capacity analysis provides a design framework for planned communities by identifying areas where development can occur and by indicating limitations imposed by resource concerns. The analysis is usually based on ranges and estimates that define development limitations. Nevertheless, some have criticized the carrying capacity approach. They view it as an improper application of physical determinism that places finite limits or thresholds on physical development (Schneider et al. 1978, 9). The carrying capacity of the natural environment is also difficult to measure, and terms like "significant degradation" that set limits on natural resource impacts make it difficult to provide consistent reviews. Infrastructures can usually be improved, and planned communities often build their own infrastructure.

Landscaping

Landscaping is a major design element, and the relationships between buildings, outdoor space, and landscaping are critical in the design of planned communities. The relationships determine project character, and thus have a major influence on design. There is always more or less of a balance between buildings and landscape masses. Landscaping can be more or less dominant in a planned community, and can either camouflage or emphasize project elements and architecture (Kendig and Keast 2010).

The design decisions implicit in landscape design are apparent from the use of landscape in the new town of Columbia, Maryland, which is an example of a dominant landscape:

> The villages are divided by this open space network rather than by roads ... Even within villages, smaller areas are divided by wooded paths, stream beds, and parks in a pattern ... described as the open space "mortar" in the "stone wall" of development. This took advantage of the strengths of the rural landscape but made the shape of each neighborhood and village difficult to perceive from the ground (Forsyth 2005, 131).

Zoning ordinances contain landscaping requirements for all developments that apply to different types of uses, streetscapes, parking and vehicular areas, and buffer areas. The ordinances apply to planned communities unless the planned community regulations address landscaping. Requirements for landscaping in buffer areas are a typical example, and there may also be landscaping requirements for different parts of a planned community project such as town centers and parking areas. These are detailed requirements that specify quantitatively the landscaping that is expected. Plant and tree types as well as spacing and setback requirements are often included. Design guidelines and manuals for planned communities may also contain landscaping requirements, and landscaping concerns may appear as one of the criteria for the approval of planned communities. The Somerville ordinance quoted earlier, for example, requires "consistency" in landscaping and the framing of public open space (Somerville, Massachusetts 1990, § 16.7).

Circulation Systems, Streets, Roads, and Other Infrastructure

A design decision on street and road patterns in planned communities is a critical element in defining the character of the community. There are currently three major patterns in use: gridiron (or grid), radial, and curvilinear (Kendig and Keast 2010). Curvilinear patterns often use a loops-and-culs-de-sac design in which loop-system neighborhoods are attached to adjacent loop systems. This model has been criticized for the isolation it creates, the lack of connectivity with adjacent areas, the incompatibility with public transit, and traffic congestion caused by fewer access points for residents who are trapped in culs-de-sac. Curvilinear patterns also emphasize the automobile at the expense of other transit modes.

Culs-de-sac can create a connectivity problem, especially in smaller developments, because they limit direct connections between neighborhoods. At a larger scale, a developer can insure connectivity by controlling the road layout for the entire area. This was not a problem prior to the Second World War, when urban development usually used a gridiron, or grid, of through streets in which there was full connectivity from one area to another, primarily because there was little opposition to connections. The rise in citizen involvement has prevented grids from being extended. Newer development models, notably the model proclaimed by the New Urbanism movement, advocate a return to the gridiron model, though with an emphasis on neighborhood character.

Planned community regulations may attempt to ensure adequate connectivity by requiring a connectivity index and by requiring fixed block lengths. A connectivity index is calculated by dividing the number of street links, which are street sections, by the number of nodes, which are intersections or culs-de-sac (Mandelker 2007, 76). This approach works well for large-scale projects that have enough connections to make the index meaningful.

Another issue is whether to separate pedestrian from vehicular traffic. New Urbanism models attempt to accommodate both. Earlier development models, such as the plan for the Radburn, New Jersey, community, separated pedestrian from vehicular traffic through a system of inner walkways. This

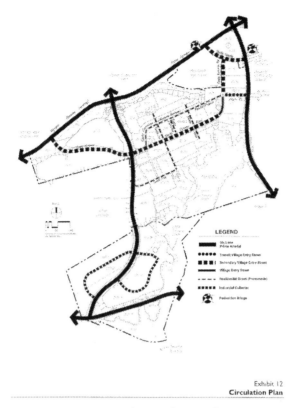

Exhibit 12
Circulation Plan

Otay Ranch Circulation Plan
Chula Vista, California

type of separation is no longer common, but newer project designs try to minimize dependence on vehicle traffic for shopping, office, and other areas by achieving better walkability, bikeability, and transit compatibility.

Though decisions on the street and road system for a planned community have a major impact on design, they are often made independently of the design review process through traffic impact studies that consider the effect of internal road networks on exit points, their relationship to area-wide collector or arterial roads, and their relationship to a master thoroughfare plan. Many elements of street and road design are mandated by state law or other ordinances and may not be modified within planned communities. These mandates usually appear in subdivision ordinances, reflect concerns for access by response vehicles, and create wider streets and culs-de-sac than project designers prefer. Negotiations to allow exceptions are necessary. These negotiations can be difficult and are not always successful, though this may be changing as interest in narrower streets and traffic-calming measures have set the stage for greater acceptance of reduced width and curvature standards.

The same point can be made about public works systems for water, sanitation, and drainage. Requirements for these public facilities are based on engineering standards that make design issues secondary, though design issues can be made more important. Stormwater runoff, for example, can be handled in different ways with different design impacts. Solutions can include a pond to retain stormwater, or the planting of vegetation buffers to absorb and slow stormwater runoff. There are also several breakthroughs in porous paving surfaces, stormwater gardens, and greywater recycling that can deal with this problem.

STREETSCAPES AND PARKING

Streetscapes and parking are major design issues. Streetscapes do not receive attention in traditional zoning but are an important element in design principles such as the Original Ahwanee Principles and can be included in design standards for planned communities. The streetscape is usually understood as the open space that spans from the front yard of a structure across the street to the facade of another structure.

Parking is critical, and the management of parking is an important element in the success of planned community design. Zoning regulations typically contain requirements for the number and design of parking spaces required for each use, but, for planned communities, the major issue is the location of parking facilities, whether they are on-site or structural, and where they are located in relation to project buildings. Design standards can address these issues.

SOCIAL PROGRAMS IN PLANNED COMMUNITIES

It is increasingly common to require planned communities to meet social objectives. The provision of affordable housing is an example (Mandelker 2007, 74, 88–89). One type of affordable housing program requires planned communities to provide specified amounts of affordable housing, and some local governments have community-wide affordable housing ordinances that require affordable housing to be part of all new development. An affordable housing requirement presents design impacts because the lower cost of affordable housing may create a design challenge, while the need to integrate affordable housing into the project may raise location issues. Affordable housing can be designed in and around market housing, so that the only difference is cost and financing. Providing a different design for affordable housing identifies and isolates those in the community who are least benefitted by that kind of recognition.

Another social program that planned community regulations sometimes require is a jobs-to-housing ratio to ensure that an adequate number of jobs will be available in the planned community for residents who live there. These can be jobs in service or manufacturing facilities or in retail and commercial centers. A jobs-to-housing requirement is intended to reduce job commuting and create a better quality of life by placing a floor on the number of jobs that must be available. Design is impacted by the effect on land planning and the ratio of commercial and industrial development to development for other uses. Scale is important, as a jobs-to-housing requirement is more easily accomplished in larger planned communities.

Some social measures are required by law. An example is the accessibility standards required by the federal disability law, which carry design requirements that apply to all developments, including planned communities.

Conclusion

Local governments turned to planned communities as a development alternative because they provide an opportunity for better design. The comprehensive review of a planned community through a regulatory process can produce a better design solution than otherwise might be possible. This chapter reviewed the types of planned communities that are built and the design issues they present. It then discussed the design issue in planned communities and how it should be defined, and the design framework that provides the context in which planned communities are designed. The next chapter takes up the design concepts that are used in planned communities and their project elements.

Chapter Two
Creating Designs for Planned Communities

Planned communities require a number of design solutions: a design for the entire project as well as designs at the site, building, and streetscape levels. The discussion of these issues in this chapter assumes a planned community large enough to need design solutions at the project level and for a number of subsidiary elements such as mixed-use centers, neighborhoods, sites, buildings, and streetscapes. Many of these design solutions are also required in smaller planned communities such as mixed-use communities. All planned communities need a neighborhood design, for example, and all must consider designs for buildings and their sites. This is true even of cluster housing. The chapter surveys the design ideas, concepts, and solutions that are available for planned communities and for each level within these communities. This is background material for the next two chapters, which show how these ideas, concepts, and solutions can be translated into design standards.

THE PLANNED COMMUNITY PROJECT LEVEL

The project level is a critical stage for design decisions; the challenge is to decide on the design solution that will produce a well-designed planned community. Planned communities are a break from community forms that have characterized housing development in the past (Hayden 2000). There is no set or an agreed pattern they should take, and various models have been used. The design solution must also accept the project mix and character selected by the developer, unless a local government wants to guide that decision by requiring a particular aesthetic such as the New Urbanism aesthetic or by imposing requirements such as a jobs-to-housing ratio that can affect the design of a project. The design frameworks discussed in the first chapter—such as requirements for natural resource preservation, landscaping, streets and roads, and parking—also have an important influence on design.

There is limited discussion of design issues at the project level. One of the most useful is Professor Forsyth's comprehensive study of the Columbia, Maryland; Irvine, California; and The Woodlands, Texas, new towns. She identified three models for organizing the physical development of planned communities. One is a network of cells; the second, a network of corridors and centers; and the third, a landscape frame arrangement where natural features provide a structure or frame within which other elements are fitted (Forsyth 2005, 216-218).

Only the first two models organize the built environment. Landscape frames, as noted in the last chapter, are part of the design framework that is present in all planned communities. Professor Forsyth recognizes that these organizational models overlap, and that other models, a uniform gridiron or linear cities for example, are possible. A hierarchical organizational pattern is common within these frameworks. In this pattern, the planned community is divided into developer units of residential neighborhoods clustered as villages with strategically placed, mixed-use town or village centers providing nonresidential residential uses and denser residential uses in larger planned communities (Hoppenfeld 1967, 403; Lang 2005, 67–68).

Professor Forsyth found that the hierarchical developer unit model for the organization of planned communities, as illustrated by the cellular landscape of neighborhoods, villages, and centers, is typical and has a long history dating back at least to postwar plans for London (Forsyth 2005, 218–222). She notes that developers consider the development unit model attractive for four reasons: identity, function, phasing, and community. By identity she means the creation of identifiable places to promote wayfinding and a sense of belonging. By function, she means the creation of neighborhoods that reflect the diversity of the community, where people can walk to work and to school. By phasing she means the efficient building of a project in phases to slow the creation of distinct subdistricts and communities. A neighborhood and village structure creates manageable development units that can be built one at a time. By community she means the creation of "a small-scale setting for important human relationships and institutions tied to a bounded place" (Forsyth 2005, 219). This, as she points out, is a contested concept, as studies question the ability of bounded neighborhoods to create the community interaction and identity that are supposed to occur in neighborhoods built at a small scale.

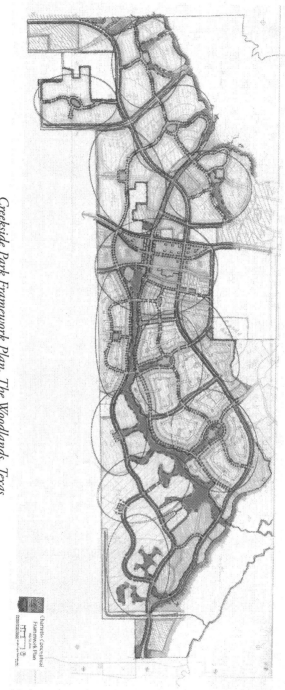

Creekside Park Framework Plan, The Woodlands, Texas
Carey S. Hayo, AICP, Principal, and Blake Drury, AICP, Senior Program Designer
Glatting Jackson Kercher Anglin, Inc.

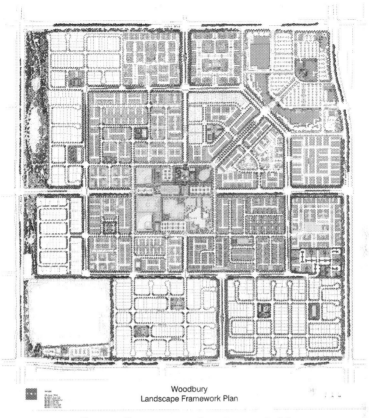

Woodbury
Landscape Framework Plan

Woodbury Village Master Plan, Irvine, California
Irvine Company

The three new towns Professor Forsyth studied are older communities, but the development unit model she describes is still widely used for planned communities, probably for the reasons she identifies. A recent study of environmentally sustainable planned communities, for example, found they also used the hierarchical organizational model (Gause 2007, 137). One of these communities is organized as seven villages with a town center, all of which pinwheel around a lake. Newer planned communities also use this model. The Otay Ranch planned community near San Diego illustrates the village concept. Each village design plan complies with the master plans for the city and county in which the planned community is located. "These plans reveal each village's unique identity and theme, and incorporate their landscape and streetscape guidelines" (Lincoln Institute of Land Policy 2005, 137).

Natural features are often incorporated into the design framework. An example is the planned community of Mill Creek, Washington:

> The basic design scheme was to take the natural constraints of the land forms as an opportunity for providing a sense of community. Along with the golf course, Penny Creek shapes an open space pattern which is the skeleton of the community ... The goal was to give the community a semi-rural character, while integrating a variety of life styles and housing types. (Moudon 1990, p. 112).

Other development models for planned communities are available. The popular New Urbanist model calls for a specified development pattern based on traditional neighborhood designs. It requires regulations that legislate detailed prescriptions for streets and public spaces as well as the placement, massing, and detail of buildings and structures. The regulations are adopted into law and strictly applied, and there is no design review for compliance with design standards. Nevertheless, the detailed prescriptions produce a particular design at the neighborhood level when a single developer is responsible for a development.

The environmentally sustainable model is another development model for planned communities. Sustainability can be an ambiguous concept, however. As applied to building design and community planning, it is intended to make an efficient and protective use of existing infrastructure, energy resources, natural resources, materials, and land while minimizing waste and socially disruptive or exclusive practices. Location is critical; for example, a location adjacent to existing transportation facilities to reduce dependence on the automobile is desirable.

The design requirements for sustainable development incorporate many features that have become accepted in planned communities such as the preservation of natural resource areas and the maintenance of a jobs-to-housing balance. The following comment summarizes the elements in a development that can have an impact on sustainability:

> The size of the development footprint, mix of land uses, density and internal patterns of connectivity have a profound influence on energy use, vehicle trip miles, water consumption, and development impacts on local and regional ecosystems (Gause 2007, 47, 48).

Designs for a planned community can take these variables into account to create an environmentally sustainable project. Choosing environmental sustainability as the primary objective that drives project development has a decisive effect on project design. It must be taken seriously and not used to mislead. A program called Leadership in Energy and Environmental Design for Neighborhood Development (LEED-ND) has developed similar objectives and is discussed later in this chapter.

Local governments must decide whether to leave the design decision to developers at the project level or to specify a design model in planned community regulations such as a sustainability model. Another option is to adopt planned community regulations that authorize a variety of design models that developers can use. Hybrids are possible for individual planned communities, especially when more than one developer is involved.

THE TOWN OR VILLAGE CENTER

Town and village centers that contain office, retail, government, and recreational uses as well as denser residential uses are a major element in planned communities once they reach a certain size. Early town centers in planned communities tended to be auto dependent and resembled the traditional shopping mall. They contained retail shops within enclosed buildings, and had large surface parking areas located next to a street or highway. Another model was the strip shopping center, which has a single clear front. Present trends in town and village center development reject these earlier forms, favoring centers that are pedestrian friendly and walkable with human-scale buildings and open-air public settings (Bohl 2002, 86). Parking is relocated to other sites such as parking structures. Mixed-use centers are common.

Mixed Use, Minneapolis, Minnesota
Lane Kendig, Strategic Advisor
Kendig Keast Collaborative

Daniel R. Mandelker

Mizner Park, Boca Raton, Louisiana
Lane Kendig, Strategic Advisor
Kendig Keast Collaborative

The scale of retail uses in town or village centers has an important effect on the design solution. Though no longer all inclusive, criteria used to distinguish different scales in retail uses apply to town and village centers in planned communities, though their design can differ dramatically from conventional prototypes. As usually categorized, the range of retail centers includes the single convenience store, the convenience center providing personal goods and services, the neighborhood center, and the regional center (Id., 81). Scale varies with the size of the planned community. Smaller communities include only convenience stores or village centers with limited retail uses. Larger planned communities have larger mixed-use centers with a variety of retail and other uses.

One critic has provided a set of design principles for mixed-use, pedestrian-oriented centers that can apply to planned communities and that can be considered as the basis for design standards (Bohl 2002, ch. 8). Defining the character of the center is an essential first step and determines how urban it is. Alternatives exist; for example, a village center for a low-density area or a more intensive town center for an urban community. Creating a sense of gravity and identity through focal points, such as a town square or plaza, is also important.

Bohl elaborates a number of design principles he considers important. He suggests that streets should form an interconnected grid, which can be rigid or modified in a radial pattern. Less rigid, but still interconnected, street layouts should not be discounted. The design should select some streets as pedestrian focused and other streets to accommodate utilities, parking garages, and faster traffic. This approach is typical in form-based codes. Aesthetically attractive relationships between street width and building height have been developed and should be made part of the design. Build-to lines should be close to the sidewalk. Blocks should be short. Walkways should be wide enough to accommodate pedestrian activity and should be unobstructed. Parking should be located to the rear or at the edge of projects, in parking courts within block interiors, in parking structures or on streets.

"The architecture of town centers and main streets must maintain a high level of visual interest" (Id., 294) and design should recognize the changing visual experience that visitors encounter. Building placement and mass are critical. The height of buildings and the extent to which they are attached to adjacent structures is a key factor in defining the center as a village or a more urban setting. The treatment of facades and encroachments such as balconies should contribute to the visual experience by enhancing the center's overall aesthetic quality and should create a relationship between indoor and outdoor space. The number of dead zones such as sidewalks facing parking areas, blank walls, and unbroken stretches of display windows, should be minimized. Bohl notes that opinions on an appropriate architectural style vary. Historic models can provide guidance, but there is definitely a need to consider modern market demands (Id., 294-95).

Desert Ridge Town Center, Scottsdale, Arizona
Darcie White
Clarion Associates

The following principles for a town center in a proposed planned community in Tucson, Arizona, summarize these design concepts:

> The town center should be planned and designed to be cohesive and interconnected, so different uses are easily accessible from each other. The town center should incorporate creative designs that include a consistent design theme and a strong pedestrian orientation that breaks down the scale and mass of larger buildings and parking areas. The town center should be oriented around a central organizing element such as a regional mall, galleria, a retail main street, or a pedestrian district. It may include a plaza, green, or square. Key components should be positioned around appropriately scaled public spaces. Higher density residential development is appropriate in and near the town center (Tucson, Arizona 2005, 21).

Village centers present similar, though less complicated, design issues. Bohl suggests a single block of large, single-family buildings adapted for mixed uses, gently curving streets and uncurbed lanes, and an informal village green (Bohl, 82).

NEIGHBORHOOD AND VILLAGE

Residential neighborhoods are the backbone of planned communities. The design of residential neighborhoods has received close attention, and neighborhood design models have been available since the early planned communities were built at the beginning of the twentieth century. Clarence Perry developed one of the most influential neighborhood models in an early publication (Perry 1929). The Perry neighborhood was designed to contain a population able to support one elementary school, have parks, be bounded by arterial streets and highways, have institutional uses such as a recreation center at the central point, have local shops and apartments on the edge, and have an internal street system proportional to traffic. Pedestrian access should be available for public facilities (Carmona et al. 2003, 114; Barnett 2003, 96–110). Perry's neighborhood model was more than a physical design template; it was intended to encourage social interaction and identity as well as to overcome the growing alienation Perry and other reformers saw in urban society. Studies suggest it has not been successful in achieving this last objective (Lawhon 2009).

Glatting Jackson Kercher Anglin, Inc.

The Perry Neighborhood
Carey S. Hayo, AICP, Principal, and Blake Drury, AICP, Senior Program
Designer
Glatting Jackson Kercher Anglin, Inc.

Perry's neighborhood model is obsolete. It proposed a nineteenth-century neighborhood of single-family homes centered on a local school and other public facilities, and is not relevant to contemporary living patterns, the use of recreational facilities, and principles for the location of public schools. Perry proposed his model at a time when the single-family home was the dominant residential type, and apartment development was in its infancy. The neighborhood school is no longer dominant, and recreation no longer occurs primarily in the neighborhood but often takes place elsewhere in community facilities. The model's social assumptions have also been questioned because the social interactions that were supposed to take place did not always occur (Bannerjhee and Baer 1984). The Perry neighborhood model failed where it was used in the Columbia, Maryland, new town (Arvin 1993, 3–4). Columbia was organized in Perry model neighborhoods of 1,000 to 1,500 homes, with three to five neighborhoods nested within villages of 4,000 to 7,500 units. Villages were focused on a middle or high school complex, a fifteen-acre retail center, recreation facilities, a library, an interfaith center, a community meeting space, and some professional office space. This was a rigid hierarchy with limited consumer choice, and the model proved unworkable. The population sizes needed to support these different facilities varied, the commercial centers had financial difficulties, and the libraries were lost. Contemporary new communities use a more flexible village model.

New Urbanist neighborhoods still follow the Perry model, though with modifications. They have similar features and place neighborhood shops and institutions at the center, but locate the schools at the edge to be shared by adjacent neighborhoods. They include a mixed-use street anchored by a corner shopping district, as well as shopping centers placed at high-traffic intersections (Carmona et al. 2003, 117). This neighborhood model has created economic difficulties for shopping centers in New Urbanist developments because their scale may not be adequate to provide financial success (Bohl 2002, 91–102).

The organization of planned communities into neighborhoods grouped in a series of villages is still common, however. Woodbridge Village in the Woodlands new town near Houston, Texas, is an early and much-studied example. The village is actually a district with a number of villages within it, each consisting of individual neighborhoods. Many of the design concepts were based on Kevin Lynch's theory of edges, landmarks, and recallable images. There is a linear, multiuse center with retail and institutional uses, which was designed before contemporary town center concepts were popular. Attached units dominate in the neighborhoods, and each neighborhood has its own school. The loops-and-culs-de-sac pattern was used, with a looped boulevard serving each neighborhood. Most homes are built on culs-de-sacs. Trails and cycle paths provide direct links to schools, communities, and shops. Economic problems developed with the commercial facilities and with the underuse of certain amenities (Moudon 1990, 45-53; Punter 1999, 148-160).

The more recent Houghton Area Master Plan adopted by Tucson, Arizona, includes similar concepts but with more flexibility, though the neighborhood definition echoes the Perry concept:

> A neighborhood is a social/physical unit based on an optimal walking radius of a quarter of a mile to half a mile. Neighborhoods include a neighborhood center, which acts as a social and recreational focal point that is accessible from all surrounding residential developments (Tucson, Arizona 2005, 25).

Other policies introduce modifications and flexibility. A range of densities is recommended with a minimum average density of four units to the acre. A neighborhood center should include a park and may include nonresidential uses. "Neighborhood circulation systems should create pedestrian and bicycle friendly environments" (Id., 27). Natural open space should define neighborhood edges. Recreational centers and an elementary school are optional in a neighborhood center depending on "the context, character, and target market segment of the neighborhood." (Id.)

Similar elements are part of the Great American Neighborhood recommended by the Maine Neighborhood Design Manual for residential development, and they are recommended to provide a departure from the typical suburban development (Maine State Planning Office 2004, 5). The manual recommends neighborhoods that are compact, safe, and walkable; that offer elements of surprise, variety, and variability; that have a network of interconnected streets; and that have a recognizable identity and boundaries, among other features.

An alternate and potentially influential model for neighborhood form has been adopted by the U.S. Green Building Council as the Leadership in Energy and Environmental Design for Neighborhood Development (LEED-ND). The Neighborhood Development Rating System developed by this group is one of several rating systems intended to encourage environmentally sustainable development. The rating system is a private certification program based on points awarded for complying with standards contained in the system. A developer does not have to comply with all of the standards and can pick and choose among them, but the number of points accumulated determines how high a level of certification can be awarded. Though participation in the rating system is voluntary, developers can be expected to seek certification in order to secure a favorable environmental rating for their projects. Earlier rating systems were developed for green buildings.

The Neighborhood Rating System contains a number of standards that can influence the design of planned communities including location and linkage, neighborhood pattern and design, infrastructure, and buildings. The system emphasizes compact, walkable, vibrant, mixed-use neighborhoods with good connections to nearby communities. The system is highly eclectic and includes some, but not all, of the elements of the neighborhood development models that have been discussed here. Because developers can choose which neighborhood standards to accept, compliance with the rating system may lead to haphazard neighborhood developments unless local governments provide more direction (Garde 2009). Once adopted by a local government, however, the rating system can be expected to have an effect on planned community regulations and on the design of new developments, including planned communities. Local governments can respond by indicating whether and to what extent they want to include the neighborhood rating system standards in their land-use regulations.

If past experience with the LEED architectural standards for buildings is any indication, compliance with the LEED neighborhood standards may be costly and therefore perhaps sought only by elite communities. Compliance with the green building architectural standards has not been difficult because many of its standards are staggeringly low. Whether the neighborhood standards will present serous compliance problems will depend on how stringent they are when adopted.

SITES, BUILDINGS, AND STREETSCAPES

Important design issues arise at the site, building, and streetscape levels of planned communities. The following design standards suggested by the Vermont Planning Information Center are usually included:

- Site layout and design standards, including standards for the placement and orientation of buildings and parking areas in relation to adjoining structures, streets, and greens
- Building height, scale, and massing standards, including standards that regulate the overall size, volume, and form or shape of buildings in relation to their context
- Building design standards, including standards for roof shapes and lines, facades and fenestration (window and door openings), materials, color, and architectural details

- Streetscape standards, including "build-to" lines and standards for street design, street lighting, trees, street furniture, pedestrian sidewalks or paths, and transit stops
- Landscaping standards, including the type and placement of landscaping elements around buildings and parking areas, within streetscapes, and for screening
- Sign standards, including number, location, height and area, lighting, and materials (Vermont Planning Information Center 2007, 6–3)

This list of standards identifies the design issues that must be considered and the physical elements that must be regulated, but does not suggest design solutions except for the mention of "build-to" lines as a design option. This is a standard that establishes the required distance between the building façade and the property line in front of it. The sign standards that are listed raise important free speech issues. Local governments may want to include them in their sign codes where comprehensive attention can be given to regulatory standards that are acceptable under free speech doctrine, and somewhat different procedures may have to be provided to meet free speech requirements (Mandelker 2004, 113-127).

Oregon Lane, Lake Oswego, Oregon
Lane Kendig, Strategic Advisor
Kendig Keast Collaborative

Design standards for sites, buildings, and streetscapes can be included in zoning or separate design review regulations where they may be limited to areas such as downtown or historic areas or to certain types of development such as residential or nonresidential development. They may or may not apply to planned communities. Graphics such as photographs and drawings can help give content to what is required. An ordinance adopting these standards usually creates a design review board and specifies design review procedures through which the board should decide whether a design is acceptable. Design approval by the board is required in addition to approval under any other land-use regulations such as the zoning ordinance.

Local governments may also adopt site, building, and streetscape standards that apply specifically to planned communities. They are most often included in design guidelines or manuals as advisory standards that supplement planned community regulations.

THE ARCHITECTURAL PATTERN BOOK

Design practice for new developments such as planned communities often uses the architectural pattern book as a way to provide design solutions for different project levels. The pattern book is an approach to design that relies on process rather than a set of design standards to make design decisions. Pattern books, which have a long history going back to ancient times, were used in the American colonial period and have been revived for use in development planning. The use of pattern books in project development has especially been pioneered by a design firm called Urban Design Associates, whose Architectural Pattern Book is a primer on this design technique They describe its purpose:

> The central message of the modern pattern book is that the character and quality of urban spaces is created through careful attention to detail at three scales: the overall plan for the development; the image of typical urban spaces within that plan; and the individual buildings with their architectural details. (Urban Design Associates 2004, 47)

These three scales match the hierarchical structure in planned communities: the project level; the town, village center, or neighborhood level; and the site, building, and streetscape level.

PLANNED OFFICE

The western entry off Liberty Pike leads visitors across a charming stone bridge, adjacent to the "Olmsteadian" community park and scenic lake, to the tree lined boulevard that crosses through the saddle to the wooded hills at the northern edge of Waterford Crest. Looking over this lake park is planned a two-story 100,000 square foot office, sited at a prominent location, facing Liberty Pike. To its rear, buffered by existing trees and approximately two-hundred feet of open space, is an accompanying 75,000 square foot research and development facility. The proposed office and R&D facility will be occupied by a single user.

DEVELOPMENT STANDARDS
•Street 'A' Setback: 20 feet minimum
•Street 'E' Setback: 50 feet minimum
•Parking Lot Setback (not including Service Areas): 10 feet minimum
•Parking: Permitted uses shall be provided parking per the City of Franklin's Zoning Ordinance. On-street parking may count toward the required parking if directly adjacent the subject parcel. Shared parking may be submitted and reviewed by the Planning Commission for approval with the Site Plan submittal. Reduced impervious surface of parking lot and the provision of code required parking only is encouraged.

Conceptual Research and Development Center

Conceptual Office

ARCHITECTURAL STANDARDS FOR PLANNED OFFICE (PO)
1. All building walls shall have equal architectural treatment.
2. All buildings shall conform to the City of Franklin Design Standards.
3. Where two or more materials are proposed to be combined on a facade, the visually heavier of the two materials shall be located below the lighter (i.e. brick below glass). It is acceptable to provide the heavier material as a detail on the building's corners, or along cornices and/or windows.
4. The facade materials for all buildings shall be natural materials, consisting of materials made from recycled products, brick, natural stone, pre-cast concrete and glass.
5. Primary facade materials shall not change at outside corners. Material changes shall occur along the horizontal line where the two forms meet. It is acceptable, however, for the change of materials to occur as accents around window, doors, or as a repetitive pattern.
6. EIFS is prohibited.
7. The use of reflective glass is prohibited.
8. Roof Materials shall be Standing seam metal roof or flat roofs surrounded by a decorative parapet consistent with architectural style of building.
9. Garden architectural elements and trellis structures may vary in materials from these standards, but shall be consistent with the architecture of the primary structures.

ARCHITECTURE   12

Waterford Crest Planned Office, Franklin, Tennessee
Landesign

Unlike design guidelines, however, "pattern books provide a systematic method for placing buildings on sites and for using specific architectural elements" (Id., 50). The process produces an Urban Assembly Kit with designs for blocks and buildings that can create diversity and flexibility. The kit identifies street types, blocks, parks, and building types as specific elements that can combine in different ways to create diverse environments throughout the plan. Flexibility is provided because the plan can grow over time, and building types can be switched or modified without changing the street or block pattern. At the middle or Community Pattern level, for example, the pattern book provides a flexible design framework by establishing fundamental design parameters such as setbacks, size, and coverage that are related to lot width and depth. Variations can occur in different locations and contexts (Id., 113). Pattern books should be used carefully, however, so that their design framework does not affect creativity.

CONCLUSION

This chapter discussed the design issues presented by planned communities and a number of design solutions for these issues that have gained acceptance in practice. The next two chapters discuss comprehensive plans, design guidelines, design manuals, and planned community regulations that can implement these design solutions. These chapters do not adopt or advocate any one particular design solution, though a variety of examples is provided to illustrate how design guidance and regulations can be written. Their primary purpose is to propose a variety of formats in which local governments can provide design guidance on the issues that are important for planned communities.

Chapter Three
Design Standards in Comprehensive Plans, Guidelines, and Manuals

This chapter builds on the discussion of design issues in the last chapter, and shows how design policies and standards that deal with these design issues can be incorporated in local comprehensive plans, design guidelines, and manuals for the purpose of guiding the design of planned communities. These documents can provide design guidance that has more depth and flexibility than zoning regulations can provide, and can include graphics such as photographs, plans, and drawings that illustrate how the design guidelines should be applied.

Distinctions should be made between these different documents. Comprehensive, or general, plans are mandatory in many states and contain planning policies for the future growth of the jurisdiction. Land-use regulations and decisions are expected to take the planning policies into account, and, in some states, must be consistent with the plan. Design policies can be one of the elements in a plan. Design guidelines and manuals are separate and usually unofficial documents that supplement planning policies in the plan and land-use regulations in the zoning ordinance. They can be brief statements of design policy or detailed design standards that apply to planned communities.

The role these documents play in the review and approval of planned communities varies. Significant design detail in these documents can provide a policy framework for planned community zoning amendments or for formal design standards in planned community regulations. Alternatively, some local governments adopt design guidelines and manuals if they know they will not be able to update their zoning regulations for some time, and need policies to support rezoning requests and variances that may arise from major conflicts with underlying zoning in the meantime. These documents are either advisory or mandatory. Design policies in comprehensive plans are advisory unless land-use decisions are required to be consistent with the comprehensive plan. Design guidance in guidelines and manuals is advisory unless the zoning ordinance requires planned communities to comply with it as a condition for approval. If the guidance is advisory, it can provide supplementary policies that decision makers can consider but that is not binding.

DESIGN POLICIES IN COMPREHENSIVE PLANS

Comprehensive, or general, plans include several elements. A land-use element that contains policies for future development in text and maps is almost always included. This element shows the type of development that should occur, where it should occur, and when. Plans can also include a design element that can address design issues in planned communities. Subarea plans for designated areas can provide more detailed guidance in comprehensive plans.

Design Concepts Plan in Franklin, Tennessee

Franklin, Tennessee, treats design issues as a central element in its planning policy, and includes design concepts as an integral part of its comprehensive plan for the entire city. An introductory statement indicates the reason for including a design element and the purposes it serves:

> This plan begins with the primacy of design quality. It recognizes that a mixture of uses at a range of densities is possible if properly designed. Community character and livability are not insured simply by planning for the geographic distribution of land use and public services. Community quality of life is determined as much by the quality of development, which is a direct function of design. As a way to plan for this issue, a series of basic design approaches is established in this plan in the form of seven "Design Concepts," which are then mapped ... (Franklin, Tennessee 2004, 21).

The design concepts apply to planned communities at the intermediate design level such as traditional neighborhood development, mixed-use centers, transit-oriented development, and activity centers. They also provide models for planned communities such as hamlets in rural areas.

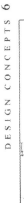

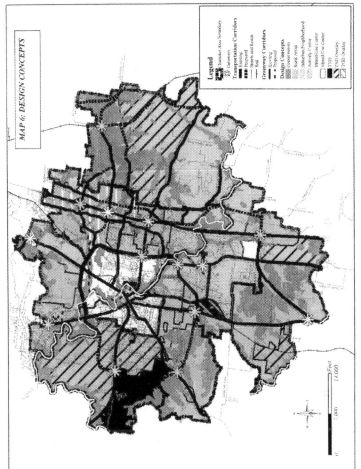

MAP 6: DESIGN CONCEPTS

Design Concepts Plan, Franklin, Tennessee

The comprehensive plan maps nine large geographic areas called Character Areas, each of which has a distinctive vision, community identity, and set of design guidelines that indicate the applicable design concepts. Special subarea plans are included for each character area. These contain additional detail on issues such as streets and lot sizes. Some of the character areas are fully developed with existing uses, and plans for these areas require a continuation of the existing design character. Other character areas are available for development, and plans for these areas contain standards that indicate the type of development that should occur, including standards for planned communities. The vision statement for the McElmore character area, for example, provides guidance for the type of planned community that can be built in that area and its design character:

> The McElmore character area will be the rural gateway into the City of Franklin. Its appealing rural and agrarian character will be maintained. Future development will take the form of Hamlets or Conservation Subdivisions to create integrated neighborhoods that have a strong sense of place (Franklin, Tennessee 2004, 75).

A conservation subdivision is specially designed so that its development will not impact or intrude on natural resource areas, farmland, woodland, and other natural resource areas that need protection.

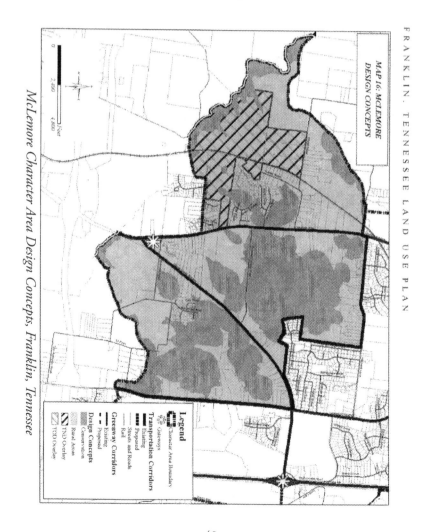

McLemore Character Area Design Concepts, Franklin, Tennessee

For a planned community to be approved in Tennessee, it must be consistent with the land-use plan, which includes its design elements (Franklin, Tennessee 2008, § 2.4.2[7][a][I]). An application for the approval of a planned unit development must also include a regulating plan or pattern book, as appropriate, within one year from the time that a concept plan is approved (Franklin, Tennessee 2008 § 2.4.2[6][I]). A regulating plan is a land-use document that is part of the regulations that are adopted for New Urbanist form–based developments.

Character Areas in Gilbert, Arizona

The general plan in Gilbert, Arizona, also includes character areas for which design standards for the intermediate project level of planned communities have been established (Gilbert, Arizona 2001). For the Gateway character area, for example, ten design policies are to be followed in the design of a village center. They require the development of a "main street" center and include design standards:

> Design a pedestrian/transit-oriented "Main Street" along Williams Field Road. Minimal setbacks bring buildings close to the street and promote pedestrian activity, window-shopping, and street-side dining. (Id.)

Resource Management Area System Plan in Sarasota County, Florida

In an effort to encourage development that provides an alternative to urban sprawl, Sarasota County adopted a resource management area system plan as part of its comprehensive plan. The system plan applies in an area of the county where additional growth and development are expected (Sarasota County, Florida). There are six resource management areas, one of which is a village/hamlet resource management area. The policies for villages illustrate how this concept is implemented. There are detailed development policies for villages and their neighborhoods, and the plan requires a surrounding greenbelt that will prevent development in the village from spilling into the country. The village development objective illustrates the development framework that is proposed to avoid sprawl:

> To prevent Urban Sprawl by guiding the development of lands outside the Urban Service Area into compact, mixed-use, pedestrian friendly Villages within a system of large areas of permanent Open Space. (Id., Objective VOS 1).

Villages must have a minimum of 3000 acres. An affordable housing density bonus is authorized.

Figure 9-1: VOS-1: Example of Village Concept

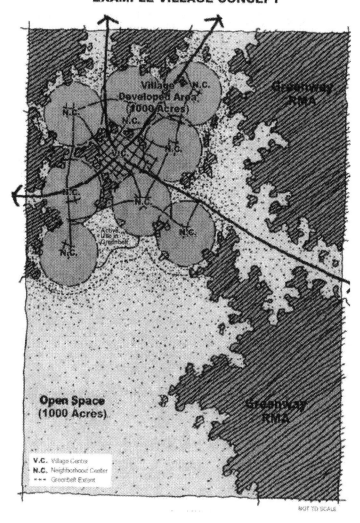

FIGURE VOS-1
EXAMPLE VILLAGE CONCEPT

Updated: 17-Nov-06

RMA-9-69

Village Plan, Sarasota County, Florida

The primary design concept for villages proposes a development model for villages and neighborhoods similar to the development models discussed in the last chapter:

> Villages are a collection of Neighborhoods that have been designed so that a majority of the housing units are within a walking distance or ¼ mile radius of a Neighborhood Center. Villages shall be supported by internally designed, mixed-use Village Centers (designed specifically to serve the daily and weekly retail, office, civic, and government use and services needs of Village residents), and the Villages shall be surrounded by large expanses of Open Space that are designed to protect the character of the rural landscape and provide separation between Villages and existing low density rural development.

> The minimum size of a Village is intended to be sufficient to support a public elementary school (Id., Policy VOS 1.2.a).

Villages must also include alternatives for pedestrians and bicyclists that provide a "distinct separation between pedestrians and traffic" (Id., Policy VOS 1.4). There is a minimum open space area requirement and percentage allocations for land uses. Hamlets are smaller development entities and have similar development policies. The policy for hamlets states that they are "collections of rural homes and lots clustered together around a crossroads that may include small-scale commercial, civic buildings or shared amenities" (Id., Policy VOS 1.2.b).

The design policy for neighborhoods in villages is a modification of the Perry neighborhood model discussed in the last chapter:

> Neighborhoods form the basic building block for development within the Village/Open Space RMA and are characterized by a mix of residential housing types that are distributed on a connected street system and the majority of housing is within a walking distance or ¼ mile radius of a Neighborhood Center. Neighborhood Centers have a Public/Civic focal point which may be a combination of parks, schools, public type facilities such as churches or community centers and may include small-scale Neighborhood Oriented Commercial Uses that are no greater than 20,000 square feet of gross floor area and internally designed to specifically serve the needs of that Neighborhood (Id., Policy VOS 1.3).

Additional policies are included, which cover the timing and phasing of development, the provision of adequate public facilities, the protection of natural resources, a monitoring program, and a transfer of development rights program. This program is intended to protect the greenbelts by providing for the transfer of development from these areas into the areas designated for development.

The Village/Hamlet Resource Management Area Plan also includes requirements for the adoption of zoning and land development regulations that establish "specific requirements" for these developments so that there will be consistency within the plan, as required in Florida. In particular, the zoning ordinance must "include the development of a new planned unit development-type zoning district that will implement the Village and Hamlet future land use designations" (Id., Policy VOS 2.3). In addition, "development activity that is designed as a Village or Hamlet" shall be rezoned to a planned unit development district and planned through a master development plan process" (Id., Policy VOS 2.4). The zoning regulations shall "establish the specific requirements of Master Development Plan submittals and the standards for the review of those Master Development Plans" (Id., Policy VOS 2.5).

Design guidelines in the zoning ordinance are required, and must establish "baseline design guidelines for Town Centers, Village and Hamlet development" (Id., Policy VOS 2.3). The plan describes the required content:

> [The] design guidelines will include, at a minimum, architectural standards, street design, transit friendly design requirements, land-scaping, lighting, access and circulation, parking, lot development standards, parks and internal Recreational Space and facility require-ments that will exceed current county standards, and best manage-ment practices for golf course design and maintenance (Id.).

The county adopted the required land development regulations, which are discussed in the next chapter (Sarasota County, Florida, Article 11. 2050 Regulations).

Sarasota County's Resource Management Area Management Plan is unusual because it specifies a detailed development framework with design policies for developments like the villages and hamlets. It is an example of a county-based design framework for individual planned communities. Major master-planned communities are not contemplated. The plan's design and development policies are more detailed than in most comprehensive plans, even specifying the acceptable mix of land uses. The plan provides for a consensus on design through the planning process that provides concrete guidance for the review of planned communities, which is intended to avoid controversy. This consensus can encourage planned community development by making the review-and-approval process more certain.

Establishing a Design Foundation for Planned Communities
By Darcie White, AICP
Principal, Clarion Associates

Planned communities are generally assumed to have a much higher quality of design than their standard subdivision counterparts due to a more rigorous approval process and higher standards for development. Take a tour of ten planned communities in the country today, however, and you will find that the quality of design—and the resulting sense of place—found in each community can vary dramatically. The pedestrian-friendly character provided by interesting architectural details and lush streetscapes in one community may fall short in another due to the presence of prominent garage doors along every block. Or the lush desert washes that have been preserved for open space, wildlife habitat, and stormwater control in one community may have been lined with concrete and walled off from residents in the planned community next door—despite the fact that they fall within the same jurisdiction. There are many possible explanations for this discrepancy in design quality: a strong policy foundation for planned communities or design in general may have been lacking to guide the planned community process; environmental protection standards may not have been in place to ensure sensitive features like the washes were preserved; or planned community criteria contained in the zoning ordinance were vague and simply left too many details to chance.

How then, can a jurisdiction achieve a more consistent level of quality within its planned communities? The chapters in this volume describe the complexities of the planned community model, some of the design issues associated with that model, and the many tools and techniques for addressing design issues in planned communities. As the reader will discover, the sheer number of variables associated with planned communities can be daunting and even confusing at times. Which regulatory approach is best? How does a town or city ensure they get the design features they are looking for without making the planned community process so complex that it stifles development? Which design features should be regulated—or not?

There are no one-size-fits-all answers to these questions. They must be considered by each jurisdiction and weighed against many state and local factors. Regardless of the regulatory approach that a jurisdiction elects to take for planned communities, though, there are lessons to be learned from the built examples that exist today. What a comparison of built examples clearly conveys is the importance of not leaving the most basic elements of design to chance in planned community regulations and processes. Planned communities that fail to address one or more basic design elements well—such as the character of the public realm, the preservation of natural features, multi-modal connectivity, building massing and form, or architectural character—are not only less aesthetically appealing than those that do, but they can be less functional as well. This is not to say that every detail of a planned community—down to the color of the shingles on the roof—should be defined before a developer ever walks through the door. Rather, it suggests that each jurisdiction should consider these basic design elements and how they have been integrated into the built examples around them as they develop their policies and regulations for planned communities—considering as much what they would *not* like to see incorporated into future planned communities as what they would *like* to see. Ideally, the resulting policies and regulations will ensure that should a future planned community be built only to minimum requirements, the resulting development will be one that reflects public sentiment about the desired characteristics of the jurisdiction's neighborhoods and not one that is looked upon with regret.

In developing a regulatory approach and process for planned communities, jurisdictions have an opportunity to establish a firm foundation of design requirements for future development. At a minimum, standards for planned communities should address the following basic design elements: the character of the public realm, the preservation of natural features, multi-modal connectivity, building massing and form, and architectural character.

SUBAREA PLANS WITH DESIGN POLICIES

Comprehensive plans are general in nature, so local governments often adopt plans for geographic subareas that provide more detailed planning and design policies. The Sarasota County Resource Management Area System plan is a plan for a subarea of the county, inserted into the comprehensive plan, that provides planning and development policies for that subarea. Local governments can also adopt plans for specific geographic subareas after the comprehensive plan is adopted. They can also include planning and design policies that can apply to planned communities that are expected to be developed in that subarea.

Houghton Area Master Plan in Tucson, Arizona

Planned communities are the preferred development options for the large, undeveloped area in Tucson, Arizona, known as the Houghton Area. To provide a planning policy for this area, the city adopted the Houghton Area Master Plan, which defines the planned communities the city wants to see in this area. These are larger than the Sarasota County villages. The plan adopts the standard hierarchical model for planned community development by calling for "a hierarchy of planning areas ranging in size and scale: Planned Communities, which are comprised of villages, which in turn are comprised of neighborhoods" (Tucson, Arizona 2005, 14).

Planned communities are given a specific design character:

> A planned community typically consists of a cluster of villages with a sufficient population base to support community-scale civic and commercial services located within a town center. Each planned community should have a discreet identity defined by its context, a system of continuous open space, architectural design themes, or other distinguishing features. The land-use mix within the overall planned community should promote a high degree of self-sufficiency (Id., 17).

Mixed-use centers within the planned community are differentiated according to the standard categories:

A hierarchy of mixed-use centers ranging in size and scale: a town center that serves as a central organizing feature for a number of villages; village centers that serve as focuses for clusters of neighborhoods; and neighborhood centers that serve residents in the immediate area (Id.).

Another element in the plan contains more detailed fundamental urban design themes for planned communities, town centers, villages, village centers, and neighborhoods. An urban design "fundamental" theme for planned communities, for example, requires "urban design strategies" that include sites and buildings "designed in context with both the natural and built environments," connectivity, pedestrian amenities, usable common areas, a safe-by-design approach, and "visual quality and aesthetics that create attractive and coherent places" (Id., 17-21). This design theme provides a contextual basis that is absent in the Sarasota plan. Policies in the Houghton Area Master Plan for town centers and neighborhoods are discussed in chapter two.

North City Future Urbanizing Area Plan in San Diego

San Diego has a long history of growth management planning, including an early plan that divided the city into growth tiers with different growth management strategies (Mandelker 1999, 805-811). The tiered growth management program has largely been carried out. One tier is the North City Urbanizing Area, which was designated in the plan as an area for future growth. For this area, the city adopted a plan that contains policies for dense, compact planned communities as an alternative to low-density development (San Diego, California 1992):

Develop two compact communities in designated areas with densities that promote pedestrian activity and transit use. The compact communities must have a relatively dense, urban character that emphasizes mixed-use development, residences within walking distance of shops and transit, and accessible public places. This pattern will be an alternative to uniform low density suburban development that creates monolithic communities and consumes large land areas (Id., Policy 4.1a, 43).

GAST HILLMER • URBAN DESIGN

- Place the front elevation of the building on or within ten feet of the front property line to maintain the continuity of the street edge.

- Create continuous pedestrian activity in an uninterrupted sequence. Avoid blank walls and other "dead" spaces at the ground level.

- Provide active building frontages with large window openings at ground level.

- Provide frequent street-facing pedestrian entrances.

- Locate parking to the rear of the buildings, or to the side when rear parking is not possible.

- Minimize spatial gaps created by parking or other non-pedestrian areas.

- At select corner and mid-block locations, widened sidewalk spaces may be provided for street furniture and planting.

- Create small-scale building frontages by dividing building facades into smaller parts.

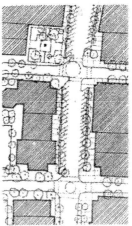

Mixed-Use Community Core Design Principles **4-3**
North City Future Urbanizing Area Framework Plan FIGURE

Mixed Use Community Core Design Principles,
San Diego County, California

Supplementary policies call for community cores, which can function as retail or town centers, organized as a gridiron or modified gridiron system (Id., Policy 4.2, 45–51). The policy has a typical pedestrian orientation:

> Design the mixed-use community cores to create high-quality pedestrian environments with building densities sufficient to support walkable shopping districts (Id., Policy 4.1b, 43).

Diagrams illustrate these policies and call for design standards for town centers like those reviewed in chapter two such as building placement near the property line, avoidance of blank walls, and the provision of active building frontages with large window openings at ground level. Similar policies are provided for residential neighborhoods. The plan provides, for example, that "[t]he core residential areas should contain a mix of housing types within walking distance of the community core" (Id., Policy 4.1b, 43).

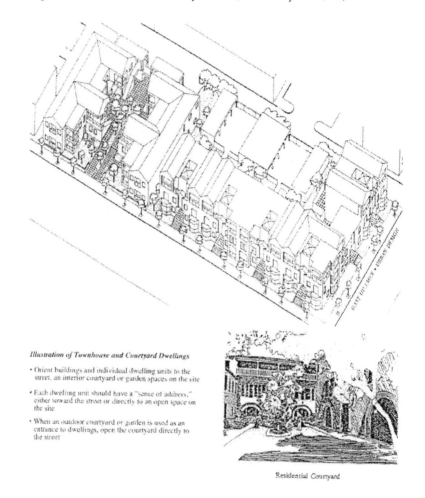

Illustration of Townhouse and Courtyard Dwellings

• Orient buildings and individual dwelling units to the street, an interior courtyard or garden spaces on the site

• Each dwelling unit should have a "sense of address," either toward the street or directly to an open space on the site

• When an outdoor courtyard or garden is used as an entrance to dwellings, open the courtyard directly to the street

Residential Courtyard

  Core Residential Areas Design Principles **4-5**
North City Future Urbanizing Area Framework Plan FIGURE

Core Residential Areas Design Principles, San Diego County, California

SPECIFIC PLANS

Arizona and California authorize the adoption of specific plans by local governments (Ariz. Rev. Stat. § 9-461.08; Calif. Gov't Code § 65450). The Arizona statute illustrates the purposes that specific plans are intended to serve:

> The planning agency may, or if so directed by the legislative body shall, prepare specific plans based on the general plan and drafts of such regulations, programs and legislation as may in the judgment of the agency be required for the systematic execution of the general plan. The planning agency may recommend such plans and measures to the legislative body for adoption (Id.).

Specific plans are different from general plans. They are prepared for individual planned communities and are quite extensive with hundreds of pages of detailed text and project maps that cover the entire range of development issues. Specific plans are similar to the development plans local governments approve that provide detailed guidelines for the development of planned communities. The difference is that specific plans are explicitly based on and are a part of the comprehensive plan and implement its planning policies, including any policies the comprehensive plan may set forth. Their detail makes them an extreme example of highly specified design guidance.

A zoning ordinance can authorize the adoption of a specific plan for planned communities. The San Marcos, California, zoning ordinance, for example, authorizes the legislative body to adopt a specific plan area zone for areas for which they are designated in the general (or comprehensive) plan (San Marcos, California). A specific plan for the area can then be adopted as an amendment to the zoning ordinance. This approach makes the adoption of a specific plan a legislative act. One of the purposes of a specific plan is:

> To provide a planning process for the installation, review and regulation of large-scale, comprehensive planned urban communities which afford the maximum flexibility to the developer within the context of an overall development program and specific phased development plans coordinated with the provision of necessary public services and facilities (Id., § 20.52.010[C]).

As is required under California law, the San Marcos zoning ordinance requires that the specific plan comply with the general plan, which is a requirement under California law. The ordinance also contains development and performance standards for specific plans, including limitations on density and uses, a requirement that the development be sensitive to the topography of the site, and a requirement that the plan preserve environmentally sensitive resources (Id, § 20.52.040). These standards are similar to those included in zoning ordinances as the basis for authorizing the approval of development plans for planned communities. One of the development standards in the San Marcos zoning ordinance requires inclusion of design standards in specific plans:

> The Specific Plan Text and Map shall include design standards (architecture, landscape, streetscape) which may include design themes or similar architectural treatments to control future construction of buildings on parcels covered by the adopted plan (Id., § 20.52.040[B][8]).

The Montecito Village Design Plan that is part of the Otay Ranch planned community in San Diego County and Chula Vista, California, is an example of a specific plan (Chula Vista, California 2006). Otay Ranch is a planned community of 22,899 acres for which the city and county adopted a General Development Plan (GDP). Otay Ranch is divided into villages; the development of each village is guided by a specific plan that provides more detail than the GDP. The specific plans contain a flexible, modern adaptation of the Perry neighborhood model discussed in the last chapter. The plans propose pedestrian-oriented villages that are not dependent on the automobile, with essential services such as schools, shops, and parks grouped in a village core. The highest residential density is located in the core, and residential densities decrease toward the perimeter (Id., I–2).

The Montecito Village Design Plan, which has 873 pages, is an example of a specific plan for a village. Its development model is a transit-oriented linear village with a core extending in an east-west direction. Well-distributed pedestrian links serve land uses in the core as well as the large surrounding residential neighborhoods. In the eastern section, neighboring areas outside the village combine with the village to provide the synergy and population to support a transit-oriented, community-serving town center (Id., II–27). Additional policies detail circulation; grading; parks, recreation, open space, and trails; community purpose; and public facilities. A separate section shows how the Village Design Plan complies with the General Development Plan (Id., IX-132 to IX-154).

Design Guidelines and Manuals

Design guidelines and manuals are another alternative for providing design standards. They are often adopted for downtown or historic areas or areas of the community that require design attention such as commercial corridors. Design guidelines and manuals are also adopted for certain types of development, including residential, nonresidential, and mixed-use developments, and can include or be limited to planned communities. The detail provided in guidelines and manuals varies from general policy statements on design to detailed design prescriptions.

A local government may want to provide authority in the zoning ordinance for the adoption of design guidelines and manuals. One way of doing this is to authorize the preparation of design guidelines or manuals that further the design objectives in the statement of purpose for the ordinance:

> The [name agency] [may *or* shall] prepare [design guidelines *or* a design manual] containing design standards for planned communities that further the design objectives contained in the statement of purpose for this ordinance.

Design Guidelines in Scottsdale, Arizona

An extensive design guideline program exists in Scottsdale, Arizona. One of its primary purposes is to protect the Sonoran Desert environment in which the city is located through guidelines such as the city's Sensitive Design Guidelines (Scottsdale, Arizona 2001b). Though these are not comprehensive design guidelines for planned communities, they do apply to planned community projects. Achieving architectural quality is an important purpose. Guideline eight, for example, states that "buildings should be designed with a logical hierarchy of masses to control the visual impact of a building's height and size [and] to highlight important building volumes and features, such as the building entry."

Additional design guidance is provided by the Architecture Design Guidelines that supplement the Sensitive Design Guidelines. An example is the following statement of purpose for commercial/retail development that is intended to encourage development with quality architectural character:

> The intent of the architectural guidelines is to ensure a base level of quality architecture that is responsive to its context and builds upon the aesthetic identity of the community rather than a design solution(s) that is based on a standardized formula or market proto-

type superimposed on the selected site. Over time, certain projects and landmark buildings begin to define the dominant character of an area. Not all buildings in the surrounding area contribute equally to the area character and each example should be weighed against the balance of all other projects. The intent of the architectural guidelines is to encourage proposals that will fit within and contribute to the established or planned architectural character and context of a specific area. Areas with little, no or poor immediate context should expand the area of influence to identify the architectural context or establish a new design vocabulary consistent with the Scottsdale Sensitive Design Principles (Scottsdale, Arizona Various Dates, 9).

The commercial/retail Architectural Design Guidelines also include typical design elements for town centers, including guidelines for building mass, pedestrian frontages, materials and color. A climate response guideline is included, as well as guidelines for landscape design, parking, and lighting. There are separate design standards for restaurants, gas stations, and convenience stores.

Guidelines for Building Sites, Buildings, and Streetscapes

In all planned communities, design guidance at the site level for building sites, buildings, and streetscapes is important. A list of the design features that should be covered in these guidelines is included in chapter two. Guidelines can cover all of these features, or they can be more limited in scope. They can apply to all types of development but may be more limited because each type of development has different design problems.

Guidelines for residential and nonresidential development adopted by Arcadia, California, are an example of limited guidelines. One set of guidelines applies to commercial and industrial development (Arcadia, California 2002). Another set applies to single-family residential projects (Arcadia, California 2009). Both are applied through a design review process, and both contain graphics. The design objectives of the guidelines are:

1. Provide guidance for the orderly development of the City and promote high-quality development.
2. Allow diversity of style while promoting the positive design characteristics existing throughout the City.
3. Encourage excellence in architectural design that:

    A. Enhances the visual environment and character of the community;

    B. Preserves and protects property values;

    C. Is sensitive to both the site and its surroundings; and

    D. Has been carefully considered and conveys a sense of balance, integrity, and character (Id. 4).

The guidelines cover the following topics: site planning, entry, massing, roofs, facade design, detail, materials and colors, landscape and architecture, and fences and walls.

Residential Design Guidelines adopted by the village of Plainfield, Illinois, are an example of design guidelines for residential developments in planned communities (Plainfield Illinois, 2005). They require processing as a planned-unit development for all developments of more than twenty acres or more than fifty dwelling units. For these projects, they provide design guidance for single-family, multifamily, and accompanying nonresidential retail development. Purpose statements set out design objectives and provide compliance flexibility. For residential development, for example, the purpose statement provides the following guidelines:

> New developments must place considerable emphasis on the relationship between buildings, streets, and dedicated open space. Neighborhoods developed under these guidelines should place significant importance on the designation of public open space and on the provision of sidewalks, footpaths, and trails in an effort to foster a pedestrian friendly community atmosphere: this is one of the key elements of good residential design that distinguishes a good neighborhood from "just another subdivision" (Id., 6).

The nonresidential development purpose statement provides:

> These guidelines are intended to provide a framework for future retail developments. This framework requires a basic level of architectural variety, compatibility of scale with surrounding uses, pedestrian and bicycle access, and recognition of the historical context of the Village of Plainfield. This framework is not to be interpreted as limiting architectural or planning creativity. Rather it is the Village of Plainfield's desire that these guidelines will serve to promote commercial development that is both aesthetically and commercially successful. However, in the case of "big box" centers,

a clean, simple design, which minimizes the sense of bulk, is preferred (Id., 19).

Detailed guidelines that carry out the intent of the purpose statements are included for each type of development.

Plainfield supplements these guidelines with extensive, detailed Residential Design and Planning Guidelines for Planned Unit Developments and Annexations (Plainfield, Illinois 2005). These recommend a variety of residential neighborhood designs, including traditional neighborhood development. They also require the submission of a pattern book, which is discussed in chapter two, as part of the planning process (Id., 11). A pattern book is defined as a "book prepared by the developer/builders design consultants that illustrates the proposed architectural theme, land planning, landscape, and any other provisions of the proposed development" (Id., 2). The Guidelines explain that a pattern book is required to provide "graphic architectural detail" for the homes that are proposed for the development (Id., 11). Brief summaries of the residential architectural styles typical of the community are provided (Id., 6–10). This use of a pattern book can also be adapted for larger, multicentered planned communities.

Design Manuals

Design manuals are another alternative for providing design policies as well as detailed design guidance for building sites, buildings, and streetscapes. Like design guidelines, they can apply only to planned communities or can include them in the developments to which they do apply. Manuals are usually more extensive and detailed than design guidelines. Manuals are often advisory, but their policies and standards may be made mandatory if compliance with them is a condition to the approval of a planned community. They may specify project development models. For example, the Chula Vista, California, design manual policy encourages the clustering of multi-family units (Chula Vista, California 1994, II-3). Design manuals may also be limited to or focus on sites, buildings, and streetscapes, and may provide detailed standards for the design features as listed in chapter two.

Sparks, Nevada, has successfully used an extensive design manual for its planned communities. The manual covers a wide range of design issues (Sparks, Nevada 2004). The manual makes its design standards binding:

> The design standards in this manual are a companion document to the zoning ordinance and are intended to regulate and restrict projects subject to review and approval under the City's Zoning

Regulations … The design standards apply to all projects subject to review and approval in compliance with the provisions of the zoning ordinance (Id., 1–2).

Flexibility in the application of the design standards is intended. Examples in designs and materials are meant to be illustrative, and developers may "demonstrate how an alternative solution will better the proposed projects design and still provide conformance of the project to meet the intent of the applicable subsection" (Id.).

The standards are primarily qualitative but can also be quantitative. There are separate chapters for single-family detached, multifamily, and attached single-family, and nonresidential development. There is also a separate chapter that provides Basic Slope Grading Standards, a problem usually covered by a separate ordinance. Each chapter contains sections on site planning, parking and circulation, landscaping, and architectural design. The standards apply primarily to sites, buildings, and streetscapes, but a limited number cover architectural design.

The chapter on Nonresidential Design Standards, as an example, first lists seven criteria the city will consider in its review of nonresidential development:

- Preservation and/or treatment of natural features
- Compatibility with surrounding uses
- Relationship to transit corridors
- Proportional size, mix and arrangement of buildings
- Placement and orientation of parking; and
- Provisions of amenities (landscaping, plazas, pedestrian friendly environment, etc.)
- Overall site circulation of vehicles and pedestrians (Id., 3-1)

There are four sections of design standards in the chapter: site planning, parking and circulation, landscape, and architectural standards for compatibility and context.

The building placement standards that are part of the site planning standards are illustrative. They require that development sites three acres or larger should have, "a minimum 15% of the total primary building frontage … be located at or near the front setback line" (Id., 3–2). They also require that "active building elevations with public access or windows shall face public streets" (Id., 3-3). A captioned illustration states that this standard precludes blank walls. This standard reflects the design principles for town centers that were discussed in chapter two.

Architectural details are covered by the compatibility and context standards. Roof standards are an example and require typical treatments:

> The visible roof profile line shall not continuously run more than 150 feet. Methods to change the roof profile include horizontal and vertical offsets, jogging and varying parapets, roof overhangs, or similar design elements (Id., 3-14).

Another standard deals with colors and emphasizes that color "should be carefully considered in relation to the overall design of the building" (Id., 3-15). Overuse of intense colors is to be avoided, and "subdued colors are recommended for overall color scheme" (Id.). Similar architectural standards apply to multifamily/attached single-family development. No specific architectural style is required, but the architecture must be complementary (Id., 5-4).

Single-Family Detached Development design standards are similar and require variety in development patterns within a subdivision to avoid monotony. Two techniques from a list of techniques must be used to achieve variety. These techniques include varied front setbacks, varied garage placement and orientation, and nontraditional design with an alley (Id., 4-1, 4-2).

These standards also include design principles; for example:

> Exterior elevation shall demonstrate a logical use of materials and a unified appearance. The design between the home and the garage shall use complementary materials and/or colors. The materials shall be architecturally related. Large expanses of uninterrupted, single exterior materials without window trim, plane, or color changes shall not be allowed (Id., 4–5).

CONCLUSION

This chapter reviewed the use of design plans, guidelines, and manuals that provide design standards for planned communities. They were discussed here to illustrate how the design solutions discussed in chapter two can be incorporated into design guidance that supplements design standards contained in zoning and design review ordinances. Many of the design solutions discussed in chapter two appear in the documents discussed in this chapter, which vary widely in the type and level of guidance they provide. Comprehensive plans and design guidelines can provide qualitative design principles for planned communities. They can also provide a detailed format for their development, as in Tuscon's Houghton Area Master Plan. Design manuals are usually quite different documents. They are more extensive and detailed, and often contain design standards limited to the site, building, and streetscape level. They are also more likely than plans and guidelines to contain standards for architectural detail.

Chapter Four
Design Standards in Zoning Ordinances

Design standards can be included in the planned community ordinance, where they function as one of the standards local governments consider when they review planned community projects. Design standards vary in detail. They may be only a descriptive standard; for example, a definition of the conceptual design for a planned community. At the other extreme, a design standard may provide specific detail for planned community design. New Urbanist design guidelines are an example.

Design standards in planned community ordinances present a different legal problem than design standards in advisory plans, guidelines, and manuals. Design standards in ordinances are regulatory, and compliance with these standards is a condition to project approval. A constitutional problem is presented, however, especially if the design standards contain qualitative rather than quantitative standards. Design standards often use qualitative terms such as "harmonious," "creative," or "innovative." This may present problems in some states, where a court might hold such language vague and unconstitutional. Court decisions that consider such standards are discussed in the next chapter.

There is no way around the constitutionality problem if only words are used to set forth a standard because all descriptive words are ambiguous and indeterminate. There is no language "fix" that can solve this problem. This chapter provides examples of design standards that use indeterminate terms that may make the standards vulnerable to constitutional objection. Selecting these standards for discussion was done intentionally, partly because plans, guidelines, and manuals can help give meaning to indeterminate standards, and partly because the constitutional objections are not as serious as many imagine. The discussion of constitutional issues in the next chapter provides guidance in deciding whether any of the standards included in this chapter may be constitutionally objectionable.

Some local governments do not have any standards for planned communities. This alternative is not an option. A review without standards of planned community projects is an unconstitutional delegation of legislative power. A Vermont publication deplored the lack of standards it found in some planned unit development ordinances in that state (Vermont Planning Information Center 2007, 22-2) and cited a Vermont statute that requires zoning ordinances to include standards for the review of community proposals (Vt. Stat. Ann. Tit. 24, § 4417[c][4]). Other states also have statutes that require that zoning ordinances provide standards for the review of planned community proposals (Mandelker 2008), and local governments need to include such standards even when they are not required.

DESIGN STANDARD CATEGORIES

Two authors provide categories for what they call different types of design "policies." These policies can provide a set of categories for planned community design standards:

- Motherhood policies, which refer only to the most general of objectives, i.e., "there shall be a high standard of design," with no elaboration or explanation of how this might be achieved or be assessed;
- Encouragement policies, which encourage applicants to meet specified objectives, often very generally expressed;
- Consideration policies, which outline a range of factors that applicants should take into account when preparing a design, or which the planning authority will consider in evaluating a proposal;
- Criteria policies, which outline a more specific set of factors that applicants should take into account and, more important, which the planning authority will utilize in evaluating the application;
- Requirement policies, which set out forcefully what the local planning authority's requirements are in design terms, although this may be very generally expressed;
- Standards/policies, which set a quantitative measure that is the normal, minimum or maximum quantity or dimension that would be acceptable (Punter and Carmona 1997, 102).

In zoning ordinances, motherhood and encouragement policies are usually included in statements of purpose that are not regulatory but that explain why the ordinance was adopted. Consideration policies specify the design elements that regulators must take into account when they review a planned community project but do not require a particular design solution. For example, an ordinance could require planned community designers to consider a design for a pedestrian-friendly environment but not specify what that environment should look like. Decision makers would consider only whether the planned community design has adequately considered this design element. Criteria, requirement, and standards/policies are included as standards that planned communities must meet in order to be approved. Criteria and requirements appear to be qualitative design standards. Standards/policies are quantitative and specify a more detailed design solution.

STATEMENTS OF PURPOSE

Zoning ordinances almost always—and should always—contain a statement of purpose. These are called encouragement policies because they indicate why the ordinance was adopted and help support its validity when it is challenged in court (Mandelker 2007, 62–64). If design standards are included in a statement of purpose for planned communities, they should reflect the scale of the planned communities that are authorized. A multicenter planned community requires a different kind of statement of purpose than a cluster-housing development, for example.

Like other statements of purpose, one on design should not have a substantive effect; in other words, it should not be a requirement for planned community approval. This limitation should be made clear in the ordinance. The statement of purpose is just that, and should be supplemented by design standards that contain regulatory approval requirements. Undefined and indeterminate terms in the statement of purpose, like "architectural distinction," will not present constitutional vagueness problems if the statement of purpose is only declarative of the reasons why the ordinance was adopted, and is not a standard to be met in order to obtain the approval of the planned community.

Purpose statements for planned communities may contain design objectives for site and building design that emphasize the need for design flexibility and innovation. The following is adapted from Greensboro, North Carolina:

> To encourage the innovative arrangement of buildings and open spaces to provide efficient, attractive, flexible, and environmentally sensitive design. (Adapted from Greensboro, North Carolina, § 30-4-3.1 [A][2])

The following statement of purpose, adapted from Vermont's planned unit development legislation, is more detailed:

> To provide for flexibility and [creative *or* innovative *or* unique design] *or* [architectural distinction and significance] that will be consistent with the comprehensive plan in site development; building design; placement and clustering of buildings; design of open space; provision of circulation systems, including pedestrian circulation systems; parking; and related site and design elements (Adapted from Vt. Stat. Ann., tit. 24, § 4417[a][4]).

Statements of purpose for residential planned communities may emphasize the opportunities for design not permitted under existing zoning regulations and the need for compatibility with adjacent residential areas. The Durham, North Carolina, ordinance, for example, states that "the Planned Development Residential District is established to allow for design flexibility in residential development," and is intended to encourage "high quality design" and "innovative development that is integrated with proposed adjacent uses and compatible with existing patterns of development" (Durham, North Carolina, § 4.4.1). Here is another example:

> To provide a means for encouraging creative and innovative developments that are environmentally pleasing through the application of imaginative land use planning techniques not permitted within other residential zones with fixed standards (Lake County, Illinois, § 21–13.1[a]).

These statements of purpose emphasize the opportunity, through planned community regulations, to provide good project design. A statement is sometimes made that the design of planned communities must be "better" than what is allowed under existing regulations. What is "better" is hard to define, and this kind of statement is not needed if the ordinance contains adequate design standards.

A different type of purpose statement is needed for multicentered planned communities. This purpose statement must specify design objectives for different elements in the project. The following is an example:

> The purpose of this ordinance is to authorize multicentered planned communities that are creatively and cohesively designed and can include pedestrian-friendly, walkable town and village centers with

human-scale buildings and open-air public settings, and integrated neighborhoods that have a strong sense of place.

This purpose statement reflects the principles for town and village centers and for neighborhoods as discussed in chapter two and elaborated upon in a discussion of design plans in chapter three. These chapters contain alternate design principles for different elements in a planned community that are also appropriate for inclusion in statements of purpose.

REGULATORY DESIGN STANDARDS

The zoning ordinance may contain regulatory design standards for planned communities. In creating workable regulatory design standards, it can be difficult to articulate qualitative standards that capture all of the design elements of a planned community with precision unless the ordinance contains considerable detail, which may not be practicable. Quantitative regulatory standards are precise, but, for that reason, may produce designs a local government considers aesthetically unattractive. The pages that follow include a variety of regulatory design standards that include both qualitative and quantitative examples. They illustrate design standards that attempt to provide workable design guidance.

Basic Design Themes

A local government may want to include a design standard in its planned community ordinance that requires a basic design theme. The statements of purpose quoted earlier contain examples of design themes that can be adapted for inclusion in an ordinance as design standards. Examples are also available in the plans, guidelines, and manuals discussed in chapter three. This example is adapted from the Houghton Area Master Plan:

> Each planned community shall have a discreet identity defined by its context, a system of continuous open space, architectural design themes, or other distinguishing architectural features. The mixture of land uses within the planned community shall promote a high degree of self-sufficiency.

This is minimal design guidance that can be supplemented with more detailed design standards or guidelines.

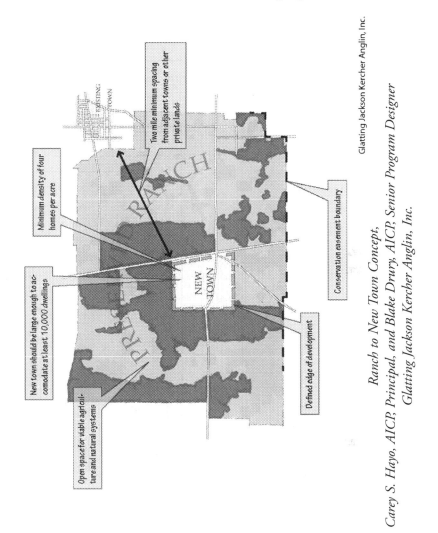

Ranch to New Town Concept,
Carey S. Hayo, AICP, Principal, and Blake Drury, AICP, Senior Program Designer
Glatting Jackson Kercher Anglin, Inc.

Glatting Jackson Kercher Anglin, Inc.

The Somerville, Massachusetts, regulatory design standard quoted in chapter one takes an alternate approach. It does not specify a particular design but requires architectural integrity in the design that is selected:

[Planned community] architecture should demonstrate the cohesive planning of the development and present a clearly identifiable design feature throughout. It is not intended that buildings be totally uniform in appearance or that designers and developers be restricted in their creativity. Rather, cohesion and identity can be demonstrated in similar building scale or mass; consistent use of facade materials; similar ground-level detailing, color or signage; consistency in functional systems, such as roadway or pedestrian way surfaces, signage, or landscaping; the framing of outdoor open space and linkages, or a clear conveyance in the importance of various buildings and features on the site (Somerville, Massachusetts 1990, § 16.7).

This design standard is supplemented by a list of specific qualitative design standards, most of which deal with problems of site development; for example, one standard requires that pedestrian transit-oriented development be maximized, and another requires that buildings adjacent to open space be oriented toward that space. Some of the standards are encouragement rather than regulatory standards, such as a standard stating that "it is strongly encouraged" that landscaped space, especially usable open space, should be "designed and located to connect as a network."

Detailing Design Standards for Planned Communities

Design standards can provide more detail. The zoning ordinance in Sarasota County, Florida, is an example. It provides extensive design standards for a hierarchy of villages and hamlets that implement the policies included in its Resource Management Area System Plan discussed in chapter three for village and hamlet developments. (Sarasota County, Florida, Article 11. 2050 Regulations). The standards are based on the development models contained in the plan, and provide a highly detailed format for the approval of planned communities that substantially reduces administrative discretion in decision making.

Collier County, Florida, provides similar detailed standards for planned communities in its Land Development Code for Stewardship Receiving Areas (SRAs) within its Rural Lands Stewardship Area (RLSA) Overlay Zoning

Districts. The standards call for a hierarchy of towns, villages, hamlets, and compact rural developments, and require an approval process similar to what is required for planned communities. The development model for towns is an example, and states in part:

> Towns are the largest and most diverse form of SRA, with a full range of housing types and mix of uses. Towns have urban level services and infrastructure which support development that is compact, mixed use, human scale, and provides a balance of land uses to reduce automobile trips and increase livability. Towns shall be not less than 1,000 acres or more than 4,000 acres and shall be comprised of several villages and/or neighborhoods that have individual identity and character. Towns shall have a mixed-use town center that will serve as a focal point for community facilities and support services ... [An interconnected sidewalk and pathway system and at least one community park are required.] Towns shall include both community and neighborhood scaled retail and office uses, in a ratio as provided in [the Code.] Towns shall be the preferred location for the full range of schools ... (Collier County [b] § 4.08.08[c][1])

Development models are also provided for villages, hamlets, and compact rural developments, and detailed design criteria are provided for each development format. Orange County, Florida, provides a detailed development model for village development in one area of its comprehensive plan (Orange County, Florida 2009).

The comprehensive plans, guidelines, and manuals discussed in chapter three contain design standards that can be adapted for inclusion in an ordinance. The Houghton Area Management Plan discussed in chapter three is an example. It contains a schematic design standard for a planned community that can be adapted as a regulatory standard in the zoning ordinance:

> The planned community shall be developed as a hierarchy of planning areas ranging in size and scale. These shall include villages, which in turn shall include neighborhoods (Tucson, Arizona 2005).

Desert Ridge Town Center, Scottsdale, Arizona
Carey S. Hayo, AICP, Principal, and Blake Drury, AICP, Senior Program
Designer
Glatting Jackson Kercher Anglin, Inc.

Design standards can also be provided for different levels of development in a planned community. Here is an example of a design policy for town and village centers that can be adopted in an ordinance:

Design the mixed-use town and village centers to create high-quality pedestrian environments with building densities sufficient to
support walkable shopping districts. (San Diego, California, Policy
4.1b, 43).

Here is a planning policy, adapted from Sarasota County, Florida, for
neighborhoods:

Neighborhoods shall be a mix of residential housing types that are
distributed on a connected street system with the majority of housing within a walking distance or ¼ mile radius of a Neighborhood
Center. Neighborhood Centers shall have a public and civic focal
point which may be a combination of parks, schools, and community facilities such as churches or community centers (Adapted
from Sarasota County, Florida (Policy VOS 1.3).

Superior Design Requirement

Many planned community regulations contain a design standard
requiring that the design of a planned community must be superior to what
can be achieved under existing land-use regulations. This standard reflects
the objective, sometimes included in statements of purpose, that one of the
purposes of planned community regulations is to achieve better design. Here
is one way to state this typical requirement:

The planned community represents a more creative approach to
the unified planning of development and incorporates a higher
standard of integrated design and amenity than could be achieved
under otherwise applicable zoning district and subdivision regulations.

However, this type of standard invites the same problems caused by similar
wording in statements of purpose. The problems can be avoided if adequate
design standards are included in the ordinance, and excessively indeterminate
terms, which are difficult to apply, are not used. How should "a more creative
approach" be defined?

Compatibility with Surrounding Area

Purpose clauses and design standards in ordinances may require the
compatibility of a planned community with the surrounding area. This

requirement ensures consistency of development in the area where a planned community is built. Here is a typical provision:

> The [planned unit development] shall be designed, operated and maintained in a manner harmonious with the character of adjacent property and the surrounding area (St. Joseph, Michigan 2007, § 13.6.1[A]).

The planned community ordinance may also include requirements such as perimeter setbacks and landscape requirements for buffer areas, which help with the compatibility issue (Mandelker 2007, 96–98). Separation from adjacent areas can also be required through the provision of a greenbelt or open space adjacent to the planned community (Orange County 2009, § 38-1382[f]). The problem is less serious in larger planned communities that can provide more substantial buffer areas at the edges, and can also be handled in a comprehensive plan with planning policies that ensure compatibility.

CONSIDERATION DESIGN STANDARDS

Consideration design standards provide an alternate strategy to regulatory design standards. The consideration strategy can be helpful for issues such as architectural style, on which there is no clear agreement and for which flexibility can be tolerated. The Peoria, Arizona, Planned Area Development ordinance, for example, provides:

> Architectural style of buildings shall not solely be a basis for denial or approval of a plan. However, the overall appearance and compatibility of individual buildings to other site elements or to surrounding development may be considered during [the Planned Area Development] review by the Planning and Zoning Commission and Council (Peoria, Arizona§ 14-33-2[G]).

Another important application of this strategy places design indicators rather than prescriptive design standards in the planned community ordinance. The design indicators identify the design issues that are important in planned community design. Developers and designers must consider these indicators, but they are not bound to a particular design solution. The local government's role is to ensure that adequate attention has been paid to the required design indicators in the design of the planned community. The difficult problem of adopting prescriptive design standards is avoided.

The design manual prepared for the English Department of the Department of the Environment, Transport and Regions in London discussed in chapter one illustrates the kind of design indicators that can be included as consideration standards in planned community regulations (Commission for Architecture & the Built Environment 2000, 15, 16). They require consideration of design issues such as character, continuity, legibility, and adaptability. Other design indicators can be included, such as natural resource area preservation, the creation of pedestrian-friendly environments, and variety in design. These indicators are qualitative, and some additional interpretation through guidelines or a manual may be appropriate. The planned community regulations can provide:

> An application for the approval of a planned community shall include [a concept *or* development plan] that has a design element that addresses all [or a specified number] of the following design indicators: [list indicators]

The regulations can then provide:

> The [name agency] may approve a [concept *or* development] plan for a planned community if it finds that the [concept *or* development] plan includes a design element that has adequately taken into consideration all [or a specified number] of the design indicators required for a [concept *or* development] plan in [cite section].

Pattern Books

Pattern books, described in chapter two, also provide a process through which designs are created but do not limit or specify the issues under consideration. The pattern book contains the design element for the planned community. A pattern book may be defined as a book prepared for a planned community that graphically illustrates its proposed architectural theme, land planning, landscaping, and any other design elements.

In one practice method, a pattern book includes an Urban Assembly Kit that designs development projects and its blocks and buildings to create diversity and flexibility. At the neighborhood and site level the kit identifies street types, blocks, parks and building types as specific components that can be combined in different ways to create diverse environments throughout the plan (Urban Design Associations 2004, 49).

RESIDENTIAL FLATS

With their location and size, the Residential Buildings create an urban-like center to the development of Waterford Crest. Large windows, generous terraces and balconies, and quality detailing make the residential buildings a grand and desirable place to live. The first floor front doors open to stoops or porches facing the streets or neighborhood parks. Units on floors above have views to beautiful scenery from spacious porches. Residents park in garages beneath the buildings, or within the internal courtyard.

Conceptual Residential Flats

DEVELOPMENT STANDARDS
• Distance between buildings: 15 feet minimum
• Primary Structure Setback from Street 'E': 20 feet minimum
• Primary Structure Setback from Street 'B','C' & 'D': 15 feet minimum
• Raised Foundation at Facade adjacent to Public ROW: 18 inches minimum
• Parking: (see City of Franklin Zoning Ordinance) On-street parking may count toward required parking
• Porch Depth: 6 feet minimum
• Stoops, awnings & columns may encroach into front setbacks to a minimum of 5' off back of curb

ARCHITECTURAL STANDARDS FOR PLANNED COMMERCIAL (PC): RESIDENTIAL BUILDINGS (FLATS AND POOL HOUSE)

1. Building walls shall have equal architectural treatment on all four sides.
2. All buildings shall conform to the City of Franklin Design Standards.
3. Where two or more materials are proposed to be combined on a facade, the visually heavier of the two materials shall be located below the lighter (i.e. brick or stone below clapboarding). It is acceptable to provide the heavier material as a detail on the building's corners, or along cornices and/or windows.
4. The facade materials for all buildings shall be natural materials made from recycled materials, brick, stone, faux stone, stucco, concrete board (i.e. Hardiboard, Smartboard) or pre-cast concrete.
5. Materials and colors shall be compatible with adjacent buildings.
6. Vinyl / Aluminum siding, EIFS and exposed smooth faced concrete block is prohibited.
7. Primary facade materials shall not change at outside corners. Material changes shall occur along the horizontal line where the two forms meet. It is acceptable, however, the change of materials occur as accents around window, doors, cornices, at the corners of the home, or as a repetitive pattern.
8. When using horizontal siding the exposure width shall not exceed 8 inches.
9. The exterior building material of chimneys shall either be made of the materials of the adjacent walls, or, match the building material of the foundation or be of stone or brick.

13

Waterford Crest Residential Flats, Franklin, Tennessee
Landdesign

Plainfield, Illinois, adopted Residential Design and Planning Guidelines for Planned Unit Developments and Annexations (Plainfield, Illinois 2005), described in chapter three. These guidelines illustrate how pattern books are used to produce design standards for planned communities, including those with commercial development (Prouls 2007). The guidelines provide direction for pattern books by including examples of preferred neighborhood development models and residential architectural styles typical of the village.

To require the use of pattern books in the design of a planned community, an ordinance may require their submission as part of the application for project approval:

> An application for the approval of a planned community shall include a pattern book that illustrates graphically the proposed architectural theme and styles, land use proposals, landscaping, and any other design elements of the planned community (Adapted from Plainfield, Illinois 2005, 11).

Franklin, Tennessee, requires the inclusion of a pattern book in an application for the approval of a planned unit development within one year after a concept plan is approved (Franklin, Tennessee 2008 § 2.4.2[6] [I]).

The planned community regulations may then provide for the approval of a concept or development plan if the pattern book complies with the design standards in the ordinance. The following example assumes that the design standards that have been included are design indicators:

> The [name agency] may approve a planned community if it finds that the pattern book has adequately taken into consideration all [or a specified number] of the design indicators required for a development plan in [cite section].

The pattern book for the master-planned community of WaterColor, Florida, indicates the design guidance they can provide for neighborhoods in a planned community. Here is part of the overview statement:

> WaterColor is composed of neighborhoods that use a regional palette of landscape and architecture. Houses are oriented to the street with deep front porches that convey a sense of neighborhood and civic responsibility. Regardless of their size, houses are unpretentious and defer to the landscape and the street. Low fences or hedges provide a subtle delineation between the public zone of the street and the semi-private zone of the front yard and porch. The predominant

public image is of shaded porches nestled within a richly textured native landscape (Urban Design Associates 2004, 93).

SITE, BUILDING, AND STREETSCAPE DESIGN STANDARDS

Planned community ordinances can include site, building, and streetscape design standards similar to those contained in guidelines and manuals. Early forms of these standards were contained in appearance codes that simply required new dwellings to look or not look like dwellings in the surrounding area without any additional design guidance. A not-look-alike standard is an antimonotony standard that is intended to achieve variety in design. Modern examples of this type of standard that can be included in planned community ordinances contain design standards that achieve variety by identifying a site or building feature that requires variety and indicating ways in which it must be achieved. Varying front setbacks is one example. Facade variety is another, and the ordinance can limit the number of identical facades on a street or in a project. Design standards can also require a facade to have a certain percentage of its length in designated features, such as arcades and display windows.

Planned community ordinances can include more comprehensive regulations for the architectural variety problem. The Orange County, Florida, West Horizon (Village) Development Code contains extensive regulations that "are intended to enhance the neighborhood character and create a pedestrian environment within each village planned development" (Orange County, Florida 2009, § 38–1384[f]). The code includes requirements for the avoidance of monotony:

- Each lot face shall include two distinct lot sizes.
- The same front facade for single family detached units shall not be repeated more than five times within each block face for both sides of any street and shall be separated by at least two lots with different facades.
- Architectural styles and floor plans shall vary throughout the development.

The ordinance then lists sixteen "mechanisms" to ensure a pedestrian-scale neighborhood that must be incorporated into design guidelines. The mechanisms include utilization of arcades, bays, and balconies; variations in color; and the use of a variety of architectural styles.

Glatting Jackson Kercher Anglin, Inc.

Limit service core height
when possible

Consistent vertical
rythym of tower elements

Integrate parking
structure into overall form

Pedestal height compli-
ments existing context

Orient entries to engage
public spaces

Coordinate transit facility
design with public realm

Design Guidelines
Pedestal Building

Effectively Mixed Uses
Carey S. Hayo, AICP, Principal, and Blake Drury, AICP, Senior Program Designer
Glatting Jackson Kercher Anglin, Inc.

Collier County, Florida, has adopted Architectural and Site Design Standards that apply to planned communities and that cover a number of site and building design issues, such as facade design, building mass, visual-interest roofs, awnings, materials, and color (Collier County, Florida [a]). Detailed design standards are also provided for specific uses. Some design issues are not included; for example, parking and landscaping.

Site and building standards may also be adopted for planned residential developments. Santa Ana, California, has adopted encouragement standards for residential design in its zoning ordinance that require supplementary guidelines:

> Due to the complexity of planned residential developments, it is illogical and impractical to define herein an exact pattern for the arrangement of group dwellings for a parcel involving two (2) or more main dwellings; however, it is the intent of this district to provide a functional and nonmonotonous orientation of buildings with a maximum of open space around each main building consisting of courts, parkways, and patio areas, all oriented so as to provide separation of vehicular traffic from play areas and recreational area[s] for children and adults.

> Further, in order to more clearly define the intent of this district, there shall be on file in the office of the planning department illustrations entitled "Guides to Planned Residential Development. " [These] illustrations shall be approved by resolution by the planning commission and city council and shall show the desirable arrangement of buildings and open space, but are not designs which must be copied in order to secure approval of development plans as required by the provisions of the Planned Residential Development District. The following contemporary site design standards of principles are designed to provide assistance to the applicant (Santa Ana, California, § 41-591).

Fifteen design principles follow that cover a wide variety of design issues, such as a requirement that the internal street system should not be a disruptive influence on the activity and function of common areas and facilities, that 50 percent of the area should be left undeveloped, and that "architectural harmony within the development and within the neighborhood and community shall be maintained as far as practicable." Additional specific regulatory standards cover streets and alleys, height of buildings, and off-street parking.

Verrado, Buckeye, Arizona
Darcie White, Clarion Associates

Thoughts on Administering Planned Unit Development Regulations
By Lane Kendig, Strategic Advisor, Kendig Keast Collaborative

Planned developments, planned unit development (PUD) or planned residential development (PRD) has been around for 50 years and it is undisputed, that they produce better designed communities. The administration or approval process is its Achilles heal. The approval of planned development is a conditional approval process, requiring public hearings, and then a vote to decide whether to approve or not. The problem is that the standards are so general that one can argue either for approval or denial. This subjects a superior method of design to more critical review than subdivisions that produce lower quality development. While this was understandable in the early 1960s when communities were approving their first PUD or PRD. In 2010, this is a costly unneeded process, planned developments should be approved as a ministerial staff review.

The public hearing and combined with generalized standards is an invitation to citizens to oppose the project. What should be a process of a technical review to insure that the planned development is superior to the Euclidian alternative turns into a conflict with the developer seeking approval and the citizens (NIMBY's) seeking denial. A good example of the failure was the Ft. Collins point system. It was a well designed system that initially worked well with council taking the planning department recommendation of the point scoring. When the citizens discovered they could challenge the point awards it became a political process. Similarly, infill is a recommended smart growth policy, but developers find the PUD process fights their efforts or results in reduced densities. A fatal flaw of this is the first rule of negotiation, put forward a position from which you can retreat to a desired condition. In forty years of reviewing and designing plats it is clear that developers and their attorneys quickly learned to ask for more than they want so as to have something to give away. The result is that the plan submission is never the best plan. Eliminating the conditional approval would change this.

Planned developments should be permitted uses, and conventional development made conditional. This eliminates the public hearing process and the NIMBY-developer conflict. The second part of the solution is to develop standards that can be checked by staff. Developing the standards offers an extreme range of options from simple with few standards to a complex array of standards attempting to address all design elements. At the simplest level, specifying a maximum gross density and minimum open space ratio eliminates a major portion of the problem. Any dwelling unit type can now be permitted because density sets a maximum and the open space insures adequate land for good design. The open space ratio should be between 25 and 40 percent for suburban sites. This range allows land for preserving resources, recreation, buffers for neighbors, and storm water. The use of these two standards creates a self balancing set of controls. If the zone permitted 20,000 square foot lots this sets the density 1.53 dwelling units per acre with detention requiring about 10 percent open space. If 30 percent of the site had to be open space the same density would be achieved with a 14,000 square foot lot. If the developer wants to use 10,000 foot lots, the open space must increase to 44 percent and a 3,000 square foot town house lot results in 79.9 percent open space. Shifting to an urban housing type then provides a nearly rural character and provides no character issue. The only additional standards needed for this is selection of standard lots in a variety of sizes from which a developer may chose.

Subdivision statutes generally contain language that suggest standards for design of roads, open space and other factors. Subdivision regulations should specifically spell out the design review required for staff and the planning commission. Neighbors feel threatened if smaller lots are jammed into their back yard. This can be addressed by a design provision that permits a review of how well the site plan buffers its neighbor. The protection of natural resources can be addressed in the same manner. If the site is wooded, a 10,000 square foot lot is superior to 14,000 because open space to preserve trees would be increased by 19 percent. As a planned development would permit any housing type going to smaller lots increases the amount of protection. The use of standards of review can be applied to the design of the street, access points, connections to adjoining property, storm water design and other elements. One review criteria is essential reducing density is off-limits.. This eliminates the ability of NIMBY's to reduce density or deny the plan and focuses on good design. For mixed use projects some additional criteria are needed to provide control over the residential non-residential mix and overall intensity.

Maximum control can be had by going to performance zoning where there are specific standards for buffer yards to protect neighbors, resource protection standards to protect the environment, landscaping, building design or other elements of the plan. One advantage of performance standards is that they set the level for all development, single-family or planned development. Performance standards seek flexibility and there are a variety of standards available that can provide greater control. While typically there are standards for all lot sizes and housing types, it is possible to provide flexibility to accommodate suburban or urban character. A new tool, modulation is needed. A modulation provision can permit the use of a pattern book to vary yard setbacks but prohibit the change from increasing the total floor area or building coverage on the lot[1]. If the developer wants small urban front yards, he should be permitted them provided the floor area and building coverage remain the same providing adequate light and air. A pattern book is a way to review for far more detailed architectural and character elements, taking the review into all the areas of concern to the community. Flexibility should be permitted to provide character while still protecting the city and the public. The use of the pattern book as a means of varying specific standards is that it is totally focused on design, again this takes the NIMBY out of the process.

Administration: Requiring Information for the Review of Design Plans

In addition to providing design standards, the planned community ordinance must provide a review process in which a local government can effectively consider whether these and other standards that apply to planned communities have been met. An effective review process requires the submission of enough information in project applications to enable the reviewing body to decide whether compliance has been achieved. Recall that the review process for planned communities may require the submission of three plans: a schematic concept plan that includes uses and densities and other major features of the project, a detailed development plan, and a site plan for individual sites. Sometimes only a development plan is required, and a site plan may not be necessary if the development plan has sufficient detail. The information required in an application to ensure compliance with design standards will vary depending on which plan is under review.

Less detail on design can be required in the application at the concept plan stage:

> An application for the approval of a planned community shall include a concept plan that includes design guidelines that provide a design and character statement and theme for the planned community, for each village, and for each activity neighborhood center with illustrations (Adapted from Clarion Associates 2004, § 2.6.5.5[D][1][h]).

More detail may be required in the concept plan if the ordinance includes design standards that require a specified project or that have detailed design standards. The design theme from the Houghton Area Master Plan quoted above is an example.

Even more detail in an application is required for the review of design treatment in a development plan, and it again varies with the detail required by the design standards. Detailed development design models for hamlets and villages such as those in the Sarasota County ordinance, for example, require enough detail in the application to show that the plan incorporates these models. Another example can be found in the Gilbert, Arizona, General Plan, which requires a design for "a pedestrian/transit-oriented 'Main Street' ... [and] minimal setbacks that bring buildings close to the street" (Gilbert, Arizona 2001). Compliance with this design standard would be required if a development plan must be consistent with the general plan, or if the local government adopts a design standard like this in its planned community regulations. To show compliance with this requirement, an application for the approval of a development plan would have to show features such as building setbacks.

If design standards include issues such as building facade, massing, and similar features, the following requirement for development plans may be needed:

> The plan shall show the floor area and elevation of representative dwelling units, nonresidential buildings, and structures. It shall also include representative architectural drawings and sketches that illustrate the design and character of proposed buildings and structures and their relationship to each other (Adapted from Mandelker 2007, 37).

This information should be adequate. Building elevation drawings would include facades, for example, so that facade design requirements can be reviewed. Other types of design guidelines may require different kinds of information. An antimonotony ordinance or design guideline that requires variety in design, for example, would require submission of drawings that show the diversity among buildings to be placed in general proximity. Streetscape design guidelines would require submission of representative drawings. Photographs and digital renderings may be required instead of or in addition to drawings, though they can be expensive to produce.

CONCLUSION

Planned community ordinances can include a statement of purpose that explains why the ordinance was adopted and design standards that prescribe the design for planned communities. These standards can take a variety of forms. They can be consideration standards that encourage but do not require a particular type of design, design indicators that guide the design process, or prescriptive standards that define the design that is required. This chapter discussed a range of design standards that can be included in planned community regulations. The next chapter discusses the constitutional issues that these standards raise.

Chapter Five

The Constitutionality of Design Standards in Planned Community Regulations

Design standards in planned community regulations can raise constitutional problems because a court can hold them unconstitutionally vague or an unconstitutional delegation of legislative power. This problem occurs especially with planned community regulations that contain indeterminate design standards, such as requirements that a planned community's design be "creative" or "harmonious." The judicial record on the constitutional issues is mixed. Some courts have struck down stand-alone design standards that are not part of a comprehensive program for regulating planned communities, but some have not. Courts have upheld design standards when they are one element in a program of planned community regulation. Even when the courts have struck down design standards, they have provided drafting guidelines that can avoid constitutional problems.

THE CONSTITUTIONAL PROBLEM

The legal issues created by design standards for planned communities vary. Statements of purpose should not raise constitutional problems if they are declaratory and not regulatory. Encouragement standards should probably not raise constitutional issues if they are only advisory. Design standards in planned community regulations that are regulatory and applied in the review of planned communities can raise constitutional problems. These standards can range from indeterminate qualitative standards to complex, multipage quantitative standards. Indeterminate qualitative standards create the most serious problem. Defined quantitative standards should not be a constitutional problem if they are sufficiently specific; for example, a standard providing a limitation on the percentage of a wall facade that can be blank.

Design indicators raise constitutional problems if they are the basis for the design process. Indeterminate qualitative design standards in plans, guidelines, and manuals can raise constitutional problems if they are regulatory. If the planned community regulations require planned communities to comply with design policies in the comprehensive plan as a condition for approval, for example, the design policies in that plan are regulatory because there must be compliance with these policies before approval can be reached. Courts will then consider but may reject arguments that the policies in the plan are unconstitutional.[1] Guidelines and design manuals are regulatory if the ordinance makes compliance with their design standards a condition for approval.

An important distinction must be made between legislative and administrative decisions when considering delegation of power and problems of vagueness raised by design standards. Decisions to approve a planned community and its development plans are made either legislatively or administratively. Major decisions about the planned community, allowable uses and densities, for example, require approval by the legislative body. Site planning decisions such as plans for circulation systems may be made by the planning commission or delegated to administrative staff. Decisions about design must be fitted into this decision framework, and design requirements are either a legislative or an administrative decision. Design decisions on uses, densities, and development concepts at the project and town or village center level probably require legislative approval. Design decisions at the neighborhood and site levels should not need legislative approval if decisions on uses and densities for these levels have been made previously. Whether a decision is legislative or administrative affects the constitutionality of the standards included in the ordinance for that decision. Legislative decisions do not require standards, while administrative decisions do. Decisions by the legislative body can be held administrative, however, if they apply to previously adopted regulations or plans.[2] In that event, delegation of power and vagueness limitations apply.

The ordinances considered in the cases in this chapter were planned unit or planned residential development ordinances that authorized the approval

---

1   Pinecrest Homeowners Assn v. Cloninger & Associates, 87 P.3d 1176 (Wash. 2004) (specific plan policies for mixed-use developments, which included design policies, upheld).

2   State ex rel. Comm. for the Referendum of Ordinance No. 3844-02 v. Norris, 792 N.E.2d 186 (Ohio 2003). See also City of Miami v. Save Brickell Ave., 426 So. 2d 1100 (Fla. App. 1983) (held administrative when legislative body had zoning power and did not delegate it).

of what this book calls planned communities. These cases are relevant to the consideration of constitutional issues raised by design standards and indicators in planned community ordinances.

Aesthetic Regulation as a Proper Governmental Purpose
By Lauren Ashley Smith, J.D. Cand. 2010, Washington University School of Law

Judicial attitudes on aesthetic regulation are critical to the constitutionality of design standards.

The majority of courts recognize that local ordinances are constitutionally valid when the governmental purpose is based solely on aesthetic concerns. Other courts hold—either implicitly or explicitly—that "aesthetics alone" is not a proper regulatory purpose; they require the local government's purpose to be based on other factors in addition to the aesthetic factor such as traffic, health, safety, and property value concerns. However, all courts recognize that aesthetic concerns can be used in some fashion to justify land-use regulations.

In the most recent comprehensive review of aesthetic regulation across the states, Professor Perlman and his coauthors, in their article, "Beyond the Eye of the Beholder Once Again: A New Review of Aesthetic Regulation," "document a movement toward greater acceptance by the states of aesthetics as a basis for action pursuant to the police power."[3] They found that the treatment of aesthetic regulation by courts can be divided into four categories: (1) states that allow aesthetics to be used as the sole basis for regulation;[4] (2) states that allow regulation based on aesthetics plus some other purpose, but are moving toward recognizing "aesthetics alone";[5] (3) states that allow regulation based on aesthetics plus some other purpose, but are not moving toward recognizing "aesthetics alone";[6] and (4) states that have definitively

---

3   Perlman et al., *Beyond the Eye of the Beholder Once Again: A New Review of Aesthetic Regulation*, 38 Urb. Law. 1119, 1120 (2006).

4   "Aesthetics alone" or first category courts include Alaska, Arkansas, California, Colorado, Delaware, Florida, Georgia, Hawaii, Idaho, Massachusetts, Michigan, Mississippi, New Hampshire, New Jersey, New Mexico, New York, North Carolina, Oregon, South Carolina, Tennessee, Utah, Vermont, Wisconsin, District of Columbia, and federal jurisdictions. 38 Urb. Law. at 1121-49.

5   Second category courts, which look to aesthetics plus other factors, include Alabama, Arizona, Connecticut, Kansas, Louisiana, Maine, Minnesota, Missouri, Montana, North Dakota, South Dakota, and West Virginia. 38 Urb. Law. at 1149-63.

6   Third category courts, which also look to aesthetics plus other factors, include Iowa, Kentucky, Nevada, Oklahoma, and Wyoming. 38 Urb. Law. at 1163-67.

decided that "aesthetics alone" is not a valid governmental purpose but that will uphold aesthetic regulation if it is also based on other factors.[7]

Courts in the first category hold aesthetic regulations constitutional when the regulations are based solely on aesthetic concerns and purposes. The "aesthetics alone" rationale is often based on the impact that aesthetics have on the community and the public welfare.[8] For example, the Supreme Court of New Jersey has upheld sign regulations that were based on aesthetic concerns, stating that "the development and preservation of natural resources and clean salubrious neighborhoods contribute to psychological and emotional stability and well-being as well as stimulate a sense of civic pride."[9]

Courts in the other categories hold aesthetic design standards constitutional when the regulations are based on aesthetic considerations combined with other factors; for example, traffic, health, safety, and property value concerns. Although these courts require non-aesthetic factors to justify the governmental purpose, this test may not be too difficult to meet. Courts have found a coalescence of aesthetics and economic, or property, values:

> There are areas in which aesthetics and economics coalesce, areas in which a discordant sight is as hard an economic fact as an annoying odor or sound. We refer not to some sensitive or exquisite preference but to concepts of congruity held so widely that they are inseparable from the enjoyment and hence the value of property.[10]

CHALLENGING DESIGN STANDARDS IN COURT

Design standards can be challenged in court if they are an invalid delegation of legislative power to an administrative official or agency, or if they are unconstitutionally vague in violation of the constitutional right to due process. Delegation of power limitations on state and local legislation are as well entrenched in constitutional jurisprudence as their basis and origins are obscure. They require that laws must contain adequate standards for administrative decisions so that a holding cannot be reached that the legislative body has delegated legislative power. There is no explicit provision in the federal or state constitutions that forbids the delegation of legislative power.

---

7   Fourth category courts, or courts which require regulations to be based on non-aesthetic factors, include Illinois, Indiana, Maryland, Nebraska, Ohio, Pennsylvania, Rhode Island, Texas, Virginia, and Washington. 38 Urb. Law. at 1167-80.

8   *See, e.g., Ben Lomond, Inc. v. Idaho Falls*, 448 P.2d 209, 229 (Idaho 1968) (aesthetic considerations are an integral part of the public welfare").

9   *State v. Miller*, 416 A.2d 821, 824 (N.J. 1980).

10 *United Adv. Corp. v. Borough of Metuchen*, 198 A.2d 447, 449 (N.J. 1964) (decided before the New Jersey court moved to the first category).

This rule is usually attributed to other principles such as the separation of governmental powers. The U.S. Supreme Court has not applied the delegation of power limitation for some time, but it is alive and well in the states. Some states apply the doctrine more strictly than others, which explains why some courts are more hostile to indeterminate legislative standards like design standards.

The requirement that laws must not be vague is based on substantive due process limitations found in federal and state constitutions. Here is the reason for this requirement:

> The Due Process Clauses of the Fifth and Fourteenth Amendments provide the constitutional foundation for the void-for-vagueness doctrine. [Citation omitted] "It is a basic principle of due process that an enactment is void for vagueness if its prohibitions are not clearly defined." *Grayned v. City of Rockford*, 408 U.S. 104, 108 (1972). The Supreme Court has explained that vague laws "offend several important values." Id. First, laws must "give the person of ordinary intelligence a reasonable opportunity to know what is prohibited, so that he may act accordingly." Id. Second, laws must provide "explicit standards for those who apply them." Id. As the Supreme Court has explained: "vague law impermissibly delegates basic policy matters to policemen, judges, and juries for resolution on an ad hoc and subjective basis, with the attendant dangers of arbitrary and discriminatory application." Id. Finally, "where a vague statute 'abut(s) upon sensitive areas of basic First Amendment freedoms,' it 'operates to inhibit the exercise of (those).'" Id. [*White Oak Property Development, LLC v. Washington Township*, 2009 U.S. Dist. LEXIS 29347 (S.D. Ohio 2009)]

A law must be vague in all its applications to be held constitutionally vague, and courts apply a more deferential standard of judicial review when considering vagueness challenges to economic regulation rather than regulations that affect fundamental constitutional rights such as free speech.[11] Land-use regulations are economic regulations unless applied in a discriminatory manner or in a way that implicates constitutional rights such as free speech, and vagueness challenges to economic regulations are rare. Courts are also more deferential when a law contains civil, rather than criminal, penalties, which may be true of a land-use regulation. These principles of judicial deference should be kept in mind when vagueness challenges to design standards are raised.

---

11   Hoffman Estates v. Flipside, Hoffman Estates, 455 U.S. 489 (1982).

STANDARDS IN PLANNED COMMUNITY REGULATIONS HELD VALID

Planned community regulations usually contain a number of standards that decision makers apply when they decide whether to approve a project. The inclusion of a design standard as only one of several standards in a planned community regulation helps support their constitutionality, and courts have upheld these standards when they were adequately stated.[12] In *Tri-State Generation & Transmission Co. v. Thornton*, 647 P.2d 670 (Colo. 1982), for example, the court upheld a planned unit development ordinance containing twelve standards that had to be met when an application for a planned unit development was reviewed.[13] Most used indeterminate language and some outlined design elements such as a standard authorizing exceptions from the zoning ordinance if justified by "design and amenities" included in the development plan. In upholding the ordinance, the court first noted the benefits provided by planned unit development regulations such as "the flexibility necessary to permit adjustment to changing needs, and the ability to provide for more compatible and effective development patterns within a city" (Id. at 677–678). Planned unit development ordinances were a "modern concept in progressive municipal planning." Standards were nevertheless

---

12   Yarab v. Boardman Twp. Bd. of Zoning Appeals, 860 N.E.2d 769 (Ohio App. 2006) (ordinance spelled out all of the elements of a project).

13   The standards were:

1. Compatibility with the surrounding area.

2. Harmony with the character of the neighborhood.

3. Need for the proposed development.

4. The effect of the proposed Planned Unit Development upon the immediate area.

5. The effect of the proposed Planned Unit Development upon the future development of the area.

6. Whether or not an exception from the zoning ordinance requirements and limitations is warranted by virtue of the design and amenities incorporated in the development plan.

7. That land surrounding the proposed Planned Unit Development can be planned in coordination with the proposed Planned Unit Development.

8. That the proposed change to Planned Unit Development District is in conformance with the general intent of the comprehensive master plan and Ordinance # 325 [the general zoning ordinance of Thornton].

9. That the existing and proposed streets are suitable and adequate to carry anticipated traffic within the proposed district and in the vicinity of the proposed district.

10. That existing and proposed utility services are adequate for the proposed development.

11. That the Planned Unit Development creates a desirable and stable environment.

12. That the Planned Unit Development makes it possible for the creation of a creative innovation and efficient use of the property.

required in planned unit development regulations, the court held, to protect against arbitrary decision making in violation of substantive due process.

Canal Street Near Town Center River Islands, Lathrop, California

SWA Group

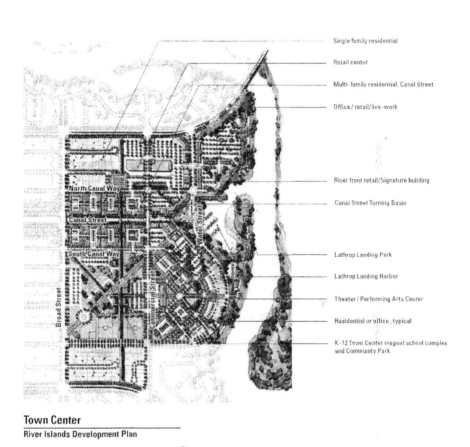

Single family residential

Retail center

Multi-family residential, Canal Street

Office / retail/live-work

River front retail/Signature building

Canal Street Turning Basin

Lathrop Landing Park

Lathrop Landing Harbor

Theater / Performing Arts Center

Residential or office, typical

K-12 Town Center magnet school complex and Community Park

Town Center
River Islands Development Plan

0   800   2000 Feet   North

River Islands Development Plan, Lathrop, Califoria
SWA Group

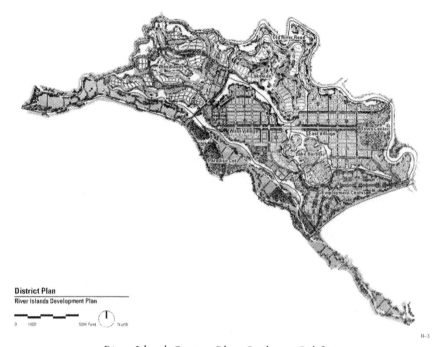

District Plan
River Islands Development Plan

River Islands Section Plan, Lathrop, California
SWA Group

Without much discussion, the court then held that the standards in the ordinance were adequate, noting that the ordinance required the submission of extensive materials that "enhance both the integrity of Council action and the effectiveness of judicial review." (Id.) This last part of the holding reflects decisions that find delegation of power requirements are met when a law contains procedural safeguards as well as adequate standards.[14]

In re Pierce Subdivision Application, 965 A.2d 468 (Vt. 2008), took a similar approach in upholding indeterminate general standards supplemented by more specific standards in a Planned Residential Development ordinance. The ordinance authorized what this book calls cluster housing. A neighbor challenged the approval of a cluster housing project, claiming provisions in the ordinance that allowed the waiver of existing zoning regulations were unconstitutionally vague. The statutes provided authority for planned residential development regulations, and the court noted approvingly that the statutory authority was adopted, in part, to "encourage flexibility of design and development of land in such a manner as to promote the most appropriate

---

14   See, e.g., Wyoming Coalition v. Wyoming Game & Fish Comm'n, 875 P.2d 729 (Wyo. 1994).

use of land," and to give the planning commission the authority to modify existing zoning regulations for these developments.

The ordinance contained general standards; for example, whether the planned residential development was an "effective and unified treatment of the development possibilities of the site."[15] These were held to be overall objectives and recommendations rather than specific standards. The ordinance also included a number of more specific standards such as requirements that the density of a development could not be increased, that only residential uses would be permitted, and that height and spacing limits in the ordinance had to be met. It also required minimum setbacks, adequate water and sewage disposal facilities, a minimum two-acre lot, and a minimum project area of twenty-five acres with 60 percent to be left undeveloped. Any modification of the zoning regulations had to be specifically set forth.

After noting that the court had to consider the entire ordinance when deciding whether its standards were adequate, the court held that "by providing both general and specific standards for PRD review, the [ordinance] strikes an appropriate balance between providing guidance to the Commission and avoiding inflexible requirements which would defeat the creativity and flexibility required to effectuate the goals of the PRD alternative to traditional development" (Id. at 475). In addition, all of the waivers for the project complied with the specific standards contained in the ordinance.

These cases are important because they recognized that the need for adequate standards must be balanced against the need for flexibility provided by planned community regulations, and because they considered the entire ordinance when they decided whether the standards it contained were constitutional. The detailed and documented process in which planned communities were reviewed also was a factor. The cases suggest that courts will uphold design standards in planned community regulations if they are part of a more comprehensive set of standards, which is usually the case, and if the process provided for the review is adequate.[16] The Pierce case was also

---

15   The court quoted some of the general standards in the ordinance:

1. The PRD is consistent with the municipal plan.

4. The PRD is an effective and unified treatment of the development possibilities of the site and the development plan makes appropriate provision for preservation of streams, and stream banks, steep slopes, wet areas and unique natural and manmade features.

5. The development plan is proposed over a reasonable period of time in order that adequate municipal facilities and services may be provided.

8. Any open space land will be evaluated as to its agricultural, forestry and ecological quality.

16   See also Rectory Park, L.C. v. City of Delray Beach, 208 F. Supp. 2d 1320 (S.D. Fla. 2002) (upholding conditional use ordinance authorizing increase in density for development projects based on compliance with 12 performance criteria, including design criteria).

influenced by the restrictive limitations contained in the ordinance and by its limitation to residential development. Standards for multiuse developments that are not as restrictive might be more problematic, though detailed standards should be possible that can overcome constitutional objections.

Design standards included in comprehensive or subarea plans are likely to receive favorable judicial treatment because they are part of a comprehensive set of planning policies. The Washington Supreme Court has upheld such standards.[17]

STANDARDS IN PLANNED COMMUNITY REGULATIONS HELD INVALID

Not all courts accept indeterminate standards that are included in planned community regulations. *In re Appeal of JAM Golf, LLC,* 969 A.2d 47 (Vt. 2008) considered an amendment to a planned residential development that would have added ten lots to a 450-acre project. A standard in the city's ordinance required planned residential developments to "protect important natural resources including streams, wetlands, scenic views, wildlife habitats and special features such as mature maple groves or unique geologic features." The court held this standard void for vagueness. The term "protect" could not mean total preservation of important natural resources because the ordinance allowed some development, which, by necessity, would reduce these resources to some extent. "How much less than total preservation qualifies as sufficient protection, however, we cannot know, because the regulations do not say ... The language of the regulations offers no guidance as to what degree of preservation short of destruction is acceptable under the statute" (Id. at 52). No guidance was provided on what might be fairly expected from landowners whose land contained "important natural resources" because the ordinance was standardless.

The *JAM Golf* case did not consider a design standard; however, an indeterminate design standard, like one that required "harmonious" development, could be considered standardless under the holding in that case because it provides no guidance to landowners. The holding in *JAM Golf* also appears inconsistent with the holding in the cases that were discussed earlier, including the holding by the same court in the Pierce case. Moreover, the holding considered the objectionable standard in isolation, and not as part of the entire ordinance. Not all cases have rejected standards like the one rejected in *JAM Golf.* Contrary to that case, other cases have upheld a

---

17   Pinecrest Homeowners Assn v. Cloninger & Associates, 87 P.3d 1176 (Wash. 2004),

requirement that scenic views must be considered when reviewing applications for new development.[18]

Constitutional problems also arise if an ordinance is written so that decision makers may ignore the standards it contains. In *City of Miami v. Save Brickell Ave.*, 426 So. 2d 1100 (Fla. App. 1983), for example, an ordinance similar to a planned unit development ordinance provided that changes in existing regulations should be based on criteria that "may include but are not limited to" a set of eight criteria. None was a design criterion, except possibly for a criterion that required the creation of a "better urban environment through the assembly of land." The court held the "include by not limited to" language made the criteria in the ordinance permissive. The local agency could totally disregard them and base its decision on other criteria or no criteria at all. The ordinance was unconstitutional. A similar problem may arise with design indicators in planned community ordinances that specify the design issues that must be considered in the design of planned communities if the ordinance does not require planned community designers and local governments to consider only the adopted design indicators when designing and approving a planned community.

DESIGN STANDARDS IN APPEARANCE AND DESIGN REVIEW CODES

Design standards are included in appearance and design review codes where they are stand-alone standards that are not part of a comprehensive set of design regulations. An example is an appearance code that has an antimonotony requirement for new buildings. These codes have a mixed constitutional history, possibly in part for this reason. A number of cases upheld this type of standard. *Novi v. City of Pacifica*, 215 Cal. Rptr. 439 (Cal. App. 1985) is a leading case. The city denied approval of a condominium project, relying in part on a provision in the ordinance that prohibited a site development permit if "there is insufficient variety in the design of the structure and grounds to avoid monotony in the external appearance." This is a simple antimonotony requirement.

The court first noted the California principle that courts should uphold vague zoning standards because they recognize the need to delegate broad discretionary power to administrative agencies so zoning may be done without paralyzing the legislative process. The legislative intent "to avoid 'ticky-tacky' development of the sort described by songwriter Malvina Reynolds in the song,

---

18   Bellevue Farm Owners Ass'n v. Shorelines Hearings Bd., 997 P.2d 380, 389 (Wash. App. 2000).

'Little Boxes'" was obvious, and no further objective criteria were required. Several older cases also upheld similar appearance standards in ordinances with standards similar to the one upheld in *Novi.*[19]

Not all courts are that accepting, especially in Florida and Illinois, where the courts have struck down similar ordinances. These states take a stricter view of delegation of power and vagueness problems than other states, and their approach to these constitutional limitations may explain their cases. An Illinois case, for example, struck down standards such as "harmonious conformance," "inappropriate materials," "durable quality," "good proportions," "exposed accessories," and "monotony of design" that were included in an ordinance and applied to deny approval to a single-family residence.[20]

The best-known and most widely discussed case striking down design standards in a design review ordinance is *Anderson v. City of Issaquah*, 851 P.2d 744 (Wash. App. 1993), which arose in an outer Seattle suburb near the Cascade Mountains. The design standards in the ordinance were indeterminate but fairly detailed. Approval by a Development Commission was required. They were similar to design standards that have typically been included in planned community regulations such as requirements for compatibility, harmony, "appropriate proportions and relationship," and an antimonotony requirement that other courts have upheld.[21]

---

19   State ex rel Stoyanoff v. Berkeley, 458 S.W.2d 305 (Mo. 1970); Reid v. Architectural Bd. of Review, 192 N.E.2d 74 (Ohio App. 1963); State ex rel. Saveland Park Holding Corp. v. Wieland, 69 N.W.2d 217 (Wis. 1955).

20   R.S.T. Builders, Inc. v. Village of Bolingbrook, 489 N.E.2d 1151 (Ill. App. 1986). Accord City of West Palm Beach v. State, 30 So.2d 491 (Fla. 1947).

21   The standards were:
Relationship of Building and Site to Adjoining Area.
1. Buildings and structures shall be made compatible with adjacent buildings of conflicting architectural styles by such means as screens and site breaks, or other suitable methods and materials.
2. Harmony in texture, lines, and masses shall be encouraged.
Building Design.
  1. Evaluation of a project shall be based on quality of its design and relationship to the natural setting of the valley and surrounding mountains.
  2. Building components, such as windows, doors, eaves and parapets, shall have appropriate proportions and relationship to each other, expressing themselves as a part of the overall design.
  3. Colors shall be harmonious, with bright or brilliant colors used only for minimal accent.
  4. Design attention shall be given to screening from public view all mechanical equipment, including refuse enclosures, electrical transformer pads and vaults, communication equipment, and other utility hardware on roofs, grounds or buildings.
  5. Exterior lighting shall be part of the architectural concept. Fixtures, standards and all exposed accessories shall be harmonious with the building design.
  6. Monotony of design in single or multiple building projects shall be avoided. Efforts should

Applying the ordinance, the city denied approval for a retail building faced with off-white stucco and a blue metal roof, designed in a "modern" style with an unbroken "warehouse" appearance in the rear, and which had large front windows. This was not an aesthetic prize, but buildings in the surrounding area were not architecturally distinguished either. In addition, the decision-making process did not rely entirely on the standards in the ordinance. "General observations" of one member of the Commission gained from driving up and down the street on which the building was located were placed in the decision record, and the street was identified as the city's "signature" street though the standards did not address this factor. Two additional plans with changes in the original building design were submitted as the Development Commission continued the proceedings, but they were not accepted.

Relying in part on an amicus brief by the Seattle chapter of the American Institute of Architects, the court held the standards facially invalid because they were vague. They did not use technical words commonly understood in the professional building design industry and did not have a settled common law meaning. "[We] conclude that these code sections 'do not give effective or meaningful guidance' to applicants, to design professionals, or to the public officials of Issaquah who are responsible for enforcing the code" (Id. at 752). The court then said:

> In attempting to interpret and apply this code, the commissioners charged with that task were left with only their own individual, subjective "feelings" about the "image of Issaquah" and as to whether this project was "compatible" or "interesting. " The commissioners stated that the City was "making a statement" on its "signature street" and invited Anderson to take a drive up and down Gilman Boulevard and "look at good and bad examples of what has been done with the flat facades." One commissioner drove up and down Gilman, taking notes, in a no doubt sincere effort to define that which is left undefined in the code.

> The point we make here is that neither Anderson nor the commissioners may constitutionally be required or allowed to guess at the meaning of the code's building design requirements by driving up and down Gilman Boulevard looking at "good and bad" examples

---

be made to create an interesting project by use of complimentary details, functional orientation of buildings, parking and access provisions and relating the development to the site. In multiple building projects, variable sitting of individual buildings, heights of buildings, or other methods shall be used to prevent a monotonous design.

of what has been done with other buildings, recently or in the past (Id. at 752).

The court also held the ordinance standards invalid as applied to reject the building's design, and it is clear that the way in which the ordinance was applied influenced the court's holding on its facial invalidity.

To provide guidance on how design standards should be drafted, the court cited two examples included as appendices in the amicus brief (Id. at 752 n.14). One was a sign objectives plan for entryway corridors for Bozeman, Montana.[22] The other was a development code for San Bernardino, California.[23] Citations to current versions of these documents are in the footnotes. The court noted that "both codes contain extensive written criteria illustrated by schematic drawings and photographs." These documents are similar in content and depth of treatment to the detailed design manuals for planned communities discussed in chapter three, suggesting that this level of detail is required to meet vagueness requirements in the State of Washington.

Later cases in that state have retreated from the Issaquah holding, however, and have adopted a more generous approach to the vagueness problem. *Pinecrest Homeowners Assn v. Cloninger & Associates*, 87 P.3d 1176 (Wash. 2004), a supreme court case, considered an amendment to a planned unit development, a rezoning and a special permit to allow mixed-use development. Fourteen policies for mixed-use development included in a neighborhood-specific plan, which was part of the city's comprehensive plan, applied to the project. They included design policies, such as:

10. To allow innovative site and building designs while providing for design harmony and continuity (e.g., coordinated architectural styles, street trees, lighting, signage and benches).
13. To provide mixed use development with a character that is less physically and visually intrusive than traditional commercial centers, districts and strips (Id. at 1178).

The court held the policies constitutional and distinguished the Issaquah case:

---

22   For the current version see Bozeman, Montana Design Objectives Plan (2005), available at http://www.bozeman.net/bozeman/planning/land%20use/2005_DOB.pdf.

23   For the current version see San Bernardino, California Property Development Standards, available at http://www.ci.san-bernardino.ca.us/DC-HANDS%20OFF/19.20/Property%20Development%20Standards.pdf.

The criteria [in Issaquah] amounted to little more than the general requirement that buildings—in their colors, components, materials, and proportions—must be harmonious with the natural environment and neighboring structures. The [Issaquah] decision chronicled the repeated efforts of one developer to intuit and satisfy the shifting personal demands of members of the development commission ... the aesthetic standards in [Issaquah] were much more general than the design criteria at issue here. [Id. at 1182]

The court emphasized that the design policies were to be considered along with seven preceding policies in the neighborhood-specific plan. It also found, as an additional distinction, that the Issaquah ordinance set up "an extremely vague building review process," but that, in this case, the city council "authorized a process that relied on a sufficiently detailed zoning ordinance in concert with a considerable number of design review concepts" (Id. at 1183).

Pinecrest upheld design standards in the specific plan even though some were quite similar to the design standards struck down in *Issaquah.* The *Pinecrest* standards, however, were part of a larger group of planning policies, and this fact, along with what the court saw as a more acceptable review process, may explain the decision. Nevertheless, *Pinecrest* is a substantial qualification of *Issaquah,* and provides guidance on how constitutionally acceptable design standards may be drafted. Other Washington cases have also refused to follow the *Issaquah* decision.[24]

CONCLUSION

Design standards may contain indeterminate qualitative terms. Standards with this terminology require subjective judgment, and courts may hold them unconstitutional if the standards do not provide adequate guidance to decision makers. The lesson of the cases, however, is that the terminology used in design standards is only one factor that affects constitutionality. The regulatory framework in which design standards appear is also important.

---

24 Cingular Wireless v. Thurston County, 129 P.3d 300, 311 (Wash. App. 2006) (relying on *Pinecrest* to uphold special permit standards for cell phone tower, including design standards, and noting that "[t]he general standards here are far more precise than the vague, free-floating aesthetic standards in" *Issaquah)*; Bellevue Farm Owners Ass'n v. Shorelines Hearings Bd., 997 P.2d 380, 389 (Wash. App. 2000) (upholding requirement for consideration of "scenic views" in review of application for shoreline development permit, and distinguishing *Issaquah* because "that case concerns the design treatment of a building, characteristics that are relatively easy to specify, as compared to scenic views").

Courts are more likely to invalidate design standards in zoning ordinances when they stand alone in a separate ordinance, but decisions finding invalidity are from strict-delegation states and are not necessarily defining. Courts are more accepting when design standards are part of a comprehensive regulatory program that includes other requirements, especially when these requirements are detailed. The reasoning seems to be that a comprehensive regulatory program provides a context for design standards that reinforces their constitutionality. Courts are also aware that planned community regulations require flexibility, and consider this necessity when they review the constitutionality of design standards.

Another important factor that supports the constitutionality of design standards is the availability of an adequate process through which decisions about planned communities are made. Good process disciplines decision making and requires decision makers to make findings that explain how the design standards they considered were applied.

This review of the constitutional issues indicates that constitutional problems with design standards need not be difficult. Courts are concerned that indeterminate, qualitative design standards may create opportunities for arbitrary decision making, but they have been willing to uphold these standards when they are included in regulations for planned communities. Supplementation of indeterminate design standards with more detailed requirements in plans, guidelines, and manuals may help avoid constitutional problems.[25]

---

25 See Brief for Respondents in Zemsky v. California Planning Comm'n, available at 2007 CA App. Ct. Briefs 19205, at 14 (Cal. App. Mar. 21, 2008).

Bibliography

ARTICLES

Barnett, Jonathan, "Charleston Annex," Urban Land, Aug. 2007, at 100.
Discusses the planning of the Daniel Island planned community in Charleston, South Carolina.

Brindell, James R., "Regulating the Architectural Character of a Community," Zoning Practice, July 2009, at 2.

Corbett, Judith & Joe Velasquez, "The Ahwanee Principles: Toward More Livable Communities, available at http://www.lgc.org/ahwahnee/principles.html from California Local Government Commission, last visited August 3, 2009.

Duany, Andres & Emily Talen, "Transect Planning," 68 J. Am. Plan. Ass'n 245 (2002).

Garde, Ajay M., "Innovations in Urban Design and Urban Form: The Making of Paradigms and the Implications for Public Policy," 28 J. Plan. Educ. & Res. 61 (2008).
Discusses degenerative variations and integrative paradigms and their effect on urban form.

Garde, Ajay M., "Sustainable by Design? Insights From U.S.-LEED-ND Pilot Projects," 75 J. Am. Plan. Ass'n 424 (2009).

Garvin, Elizabeth & Dawn Jourdan, "Through the Looking Glass: Analyzing the Potential Legal Challenges to Form-Based codes,"23 J. Land Use & Envtl. L. 395 (2008).

Garvin, Elizabeth & Glenn S. Leroy, "Design Guidelines: The Law of Aesthetics," Land Use Law & Zoning Digest, Vol. 55, No. 4, at 3 (2003).

George, R. Varkki, "A Procedural Explanation for Contemporary Urban Design," J. Urb. Design," 2 J. Urb. Design 143 (1997).

Habe, Reiko, "Public Design Control in American Communities," 60 Town Plan. Rev. 195 (1989).

Discusses a survey of design review practices in American communities in built-up areas.

Hersperger, Anne M., "Landscape Ecology and Its Potential Application to Planning," 9 J. Plan. Lit. 14 (1994).

Hoppenfeld, Morton, "A Sketch of the Planning-Building Process for Columbia, Maryland," 33 J. Am. Plan. Ass'n 398 (1967).

Discusses the hierarchical planning structure.

Lawhon, Larry Lloyd, "The Neighborhood Unit: Physical Design or Physical Determinism," 8 J. Plan. History 111 (2009).

Discusses origins and criticisms of the neighborhood unit idea.

Lee, Chang-Moo & Barbara Stabin-Nesmith, "The Continuing Value of a Planned Community: Radburn in the Evolution of Suburban Development," 6 J. Urb. Design 151 (2001).

Madanipoor, Ali, "Roles and Challenges of Urban Design," 11 J. Urb. Design 173 (2006).

Mandelker, Daniel R, "Legislation for Planned Unit Developments and Master-Planned Communities," 35 Urban Lawyer 419 (2008).

Mandelker, Daniel R, "Managing Space to Manage Growth," 23 William & Mary Envtl. L. & Pol'y Rev. 801 (1999).

Discusses growth management plans in San Diego and Oregon.

Maximuk, John, "Where Does Design Fit In?," Planning, Dec. 2007, at 42.

Moody, Jason & Andy Knudsten, "Urban Suburbia," Urban Land, Oct. 2008, at 178.

Discusses infill projects, notes must provide integrated, appealing and walkable urban design for town centers.

Nasar, Jack L. & Peg Grannis, "Design Review Reviewed: Administrative versus Discretionary Methods," 65 J. Am. Plan. Ass'n 424 (1999).

Finds that discretionary review not necessarily better than standards in Columbus survey.

O'Connor, Zena, "Bridging the Gap: Facade Colour, Aesthetic Response and Planning Policy, 11 J. Urb. Design 334 (2006).

Proulx. Jonathan, "Guiding Growth in a Bomming Suburb: Plainfield Adopts Design Guidelines," Planning, Oct. 2007, at 32.

Punter, John, "Developing Urban Design as Public Policy: Best Practice Principle for Design Review and Development Management, 12 J. Urb. Design 167 (2007).

Sayre, Nathan F., "The Genesis, History and Limits of Carrying Capacity," 76 Annals of the Ass'n of Am. Geographers 120 (2008).

Tarlock, Dan, "Fat and Fried: Linking Land Use Law, The Risks of Obesity, and Climat Change," 3 Pitt. J. Envtl. & Pub. Health L. 31 (2009).

Taylor, Nigel, "Legibility and Aesthetics in Urban Design," 14 J. Urb. Design 189 (2009).

BOOKS, CHAPTERS IN BOOKS AND MONOGRAPHS

Avin, Uri P. 1993. *Chewing the Cud with a PUD — Lessons from Howard County and Columbia New Town in Institute on Planning, Zoning, and Eminent Domain* Ch. 3. New York, NY. Matthew Bender.

Bannerjhee, Tridib & William C. Baer 1984. *Beyond the Neighborhood Unit.* New York, NY. Plenum Press.

Barnett, Jonathan 1982. *Design Formulations for Planned Communities* in *An Introduction to Urban Design* Ch. 9. New York, NY. Harper & Row.

Barnett, Jonathan 2003. *Redesigning Cities.* Chicago, IL. American Planning Association.

Bohl, Charles C. 2002. *Place Making: Developing Town Centers, Main Streets and Urban Villages.* Washington, D.C. The Urban Land Institute.

Campoli, Julie & Alex S. MacLean 2007. *Visualizing Density.* Cambridge, MA. Lincoln Institute of Land Policy.

Carmona, Matthew & Tim Heath, Tanner Oc & Steve Tiesdell 2003. *Public Places - Urban Spaces.* Oxford, UK. Elsevier.
Comprehensive review of urban design issues, including implementation issues.

Carmonoa, Mathhew & Steve Tiesdell, Ed. 2007. *Urban Design Reader.* Oxford, UK. Architectural Press, Elsevier.

Commission for Architecture & the Built Environment 2000. *By Design: Urban Design in the Planning System: Toward Better Practice.* London, UK. Department of the Environment, Transport and Regions, available at http://www.cabe.org.uk/files/by-design-urban-design-in-the-planning-system.pdf, last visited, October 16, 2009.
Excellent practice guide on design elements.

Choay, Francoise 1997. *The Rule and the Model: On the Theory of Architecture and Urbanism.* Cambridge, MA. The MIT Press.

Cuthbert, Alexander R. 2006. *The Form of Cities:Political Economy and Urban Design.* Hoboken, N.J. Wiley-Blackwell.

Dobbins, Michael 2009. *Urban Design and People.* Hoboken, N.J. John Wiley.

Duerksen, Christopher J.1986. *Aesthetics and Land-Use Controls.* Planning Advisory Service Report No. 399. Chicago, IL. American Planning Association.
Covers design review, view protection, tree protection, signs and other outdoor communication with discussion of legal issues.

Forsyth, Ann 2005. *Reforming Suburbia: The Planned Communities of Irvine, Columbia, and The Woodlands.* Berkeley, CA. University of California Press.

Gause, Jo Ellen, Ed. 2007. *Developing Sustainable Planned Communities.* Washington, D.C. Urban Land Institute.
Contains guidelines for development and case studies.

Gosling, David 2003. *The Evolution of American Urban Design: A Chronological Anthology.* Hoboken, NJ. John Wiley & Sons.

Gupta, Prema Katari & Kathryn Terzano, Eds. 2008. *Creating Great Town Centers and Urban Villages.* Washington, D.C. Urban Land Institute.
Discusses development and design principles and includes several case studies.

Handy, Susan, Robert J. Paterson & Kent Butler 2003. *Planning for Street Connectivity: Getting from Here to There.* Planning Advisory Report No. 515. Chicago, IL. American Planning Association.

Hayden, Delores 2002. *What is Suburbia? Naming the Layers in the Landscape,* in *Smart Growth: Form and Consequences* Ch. 2, Szold, Terry S & Armando Carbonell, Eds. Cambridge, MA. Lincoln Institute of Land Policy.

Hinshaw, Mark L.1995. *Design Guidelines.* Planning Advisory Service Report No. 454. Chicago, IL. American Planning Association.
Review of design review process and design guidelines.

Jerke, Dennis, Douglas R. Porter & Terry J. Lassar 2008. *Urban Design and the Bottom Line.* Washington, D.C. Urban Land Institute.

Kendig, Lane & Brent Keast 2010. *Community Character.* Washington, D.C. Island Press.

Kendig, Lane 2004. *Too Big, Boring, or Ugly: Planning and Design Tools to Combat Monotony, the Too-Big House, and Teardowns.* Planning Advisory Service Report No. 528. Chicago, IL. American Planning Association.
Discusses design guidelines for homes with examples of regulations.

Krizek, Kevin & Je Power 1996. *A Planner's Guide to Sustainable Development.* Planning Advisory Service Report No. 467. Chicago, IL. American Planning Association.

Lang, John 2005. *Urban Design: A Typology of Procedures and Products.* Oxford, UK. Architectural Press, Elsevier.

Lincoln Institute of Land Policy, Sonoran Institute. 2005. *Growing Smarter on the Edge.* Boston, Mass. and Phoenix, AZ. Lincoln Institute of Land Policy and Sonoran Institute.
Case studies of planned communities in the western U.S.

Lynch, Kevin 1981. *Good City Form.* Cambaridge, MA. MIT Press.

Lynch, Kevin 1960. *The Image of the City.* Cambridge, MA. MIT Press.

Mandelker, Daniel R. 2007. *Planned Unit Developments.* Planning Advisory Service Report No. 545. Chicago, IL. American Planning Association.

Mandelker, Daniel R. 2004. *Street Graphics on the Law* (Revised Edition, with Andrew Bertucci & William Ewald). Planning Advisory Service Report No. 527. Chicago, IL. American Planning Association.

Meck, Stuart 2002. *Growing Smart Legislative Guidebook: Model Statutes for Planning and Management of Change.* Chicago, IL. American Planning Association.

Moudon, Anne Vernez, Ed. 1990. *Master-Planned Communities: Shaping Exurbs in the 1990s.* Seattle, Wash., College of Architecture and Urban Planning, University of Washington.

Report of a conference that discussed issues in master-planned communities with case examples nationally and in the Seattle area.

McHarg, Ian. 1969. *Design With Nature.* Garden City, N.Y. Natural History Press.

Moughtin, Cliff, Rafael Costa, Christine Sarris & Paola Signoretta 2d ed., 2003, *Urban Design: Methods and Techniques.* Oxford, UK. Architectural Press, Elsevier.

Morris, Marya Ed. 2009. *Smart Codes: Model Land-Development Regulations.* Planning Advisory Service Report No. 556. Chicago, IL. American Planning Association.

Olshansky, Robert B. 1996. *Planning for Hillside Development.* Planning Advisory Service Report No. 466. Chicago, IL. American Planning Association.

Parolek, Daniel G., Karen Parolek & Paul C. Crawford 2008. *Form-Based Codes: A Guide for Planners, Urban Designers, Municipalities, and Developers.* Hoboken, N.J. John Wiley & Sons.

Perry, Clarence A. 1929. *The Neighborhood Unit,* in *Regional Plan for New York and its Environs, Vol. 7, Neighborhood and Community Planning,* Harold M. Lewis, Ed. New York, N.Y. The Committee on Regional Plan of New York and Its Environs.

Porter, Douglas R. 2d ed., 2008. *Managing Growth in America's Communities.* Washington, D.C. Island Press.

Includes chapter on urban design.

Punter, John 1999. *Design Guidelines in American Cities.* Liverpool, UK. Liverpool University Press.

Review of design policies and guidance in five west coast cities.

Punter, John & Matthew Carmona 1997. *The Design Dimension of Planning: Theory, Content and Best Practice for Design Policies.* London, UK. E & FN Spon.

Schneider, Devon M., David R. Godschalk & Norman Axler 1978. *The Carrying Capacity Concept as a Planning Tool.* Planning Advisory Service Report No. 338. Chicago, IL. American Planning Association.

Slone, Daniel K. & Doris S. Goldstein 2008. *A Legal Guide to Urban and Sustainable Development for Planners, Developers, and Architects.* Hoboken, NJ. John Wiley & Sons, Inc.

Steiner, Frederick & Kent Butler, Eds. 2007. *Planning and Urban Design Standards: Student Edition.* Hoboken, N.J. John Wiley & Sons, Inc.

Talen, Emily 2008. *Design for Diversity: Exploring Socially Mixed Neighborhoods.* Oxford, UK. Architectural Press, Elsevier.

Urban Design Associates 2004. *The Architectural Pattern Book.* New York, N.Y. W.W. Norton & Company.
A design process for project planning.

Urban Design Associates 2003. *The Urban Design Handbook.* New York, N.Y. W.W. Norton & Company.

Urban Land Institute 1998. *Trends and Innovations in Master-Planned Communities.* Washington, D.C. Urban Land Institute.
Discusses New Urbanism design and has case studies of three communities including their design features.

Urban Land Institute 2008. *Getting Density Right: Tools for Creating Vibrant Compact Development.* Washington, D.C. Urban Land Institute
Reviews a number of approaches to these developments with references to online sources.

U.S. Green Building Council 2009. *Green Neighborhood Development Reference Guide.* Washington, D.C. U.S. Green Building Council.

Walters, David. 2007. *Designing Community: Charrettes, Masterplans and Form-Based Codes.* Oxford, UK. Architectural Press, Elsevier.

Watson, Donald & Alan Plattus & Robert G.Shibley, Eds. 2003. *Time-Saver Standards for Urban Design.* New York, N.Y. McGraw-Hill.
Includes sections on the neighborhood unit, Kevin Lynch and Radburn.

GRADUATE THESES

Gritzmacher, Christopher B. 2004. *Urban Design Within the Planning Process: A Case Study of Current Practice (Block E in Minneapolis).* A Thesis Presented for the Master in Community Planning Degrees. Cincinnati, Ohio. University of Cincinnati. (On file with author.)

Zenner, Patrick B. 1998. *Planned Unit Development in the Southeast — An Analysis of Its Success.* A Thesis Presented for the Master of Science Degree. Knoxville, Tenn. University of Tennessee. (On file with author.)

Study based on survey of projects and ordinances in several local governments.

DOCUMENTS, PLANS. GUIDELINES AND MANUALS

Ada County, Idaho 1997. *Hidden Springs Specific Plan,* available at http://sterling.webiness.com/codebook/index.php?book_id=447, last visited, June 24, 2009.

Ada County, Idaho 2007. *Comprehensive Plan,* available at http://www.adaweb.net/LinkClick.aspx?fileticket=jKISyZxA5Yw%3d&tabid=259 , last visited June 20, 2009.

Arcadia, California 2002. *Architectural Design Guidelines: Commercial and Industrial,* available at http://www.ci.arcadia.ca.us/docs/adr_comm_regs.pdf, last visited, July 24, 2009.

Arcadia, California 2009. *Single Family Residential Guidelines,* available at http://www.ci.arcadia.ca.us/docs/sf_arch_design_guidelines_4-17-09.pdf, last visited July 24, 2009.

Baltimore County, Maryland. *Planned Unit Development,* available at http://www.baltimorecountymd.gov/Agencies/planning/PUD/index.html, last visited, June 30, 2009 (includes links to projects and project pattern books).

California Local Government Commission 1991. *Original Ahwanee Principles,* available at http://www.lgc.org/ahwahnee/principles.html, last visited August 3, 2009.

Chula Vista, California 1994. *Design Manual,* available at http://www.chulavistaca.gov/City_Services/Development_Services/Planning_Building/PDF/Design_Manual.pdf, last visited June 23, 2009.

Chula Vista, California 2006. *Village of Montecito and Otay Ranch Business Park, Sectional Planning Area Plan: Villages Two, Three, Portion of Village Four, Otay Ranch GDP,* available at http://www.chulavistaca.gov/City_Services/Development_Services/Planning_Building/documents/Otay.Ranch.Village.2.SPA-Web.pdf, last visited June 25, 2009.

Congress of the New Urbanism 2001. *Charter of the New Urbanism,* available at http://www.cnu.org/sites/files/charter_english.pdf, last visited May 17, 2009.

Franklin, Tennessee 2004, amended 2007. *Land Use Plan,* available at http://www.franklintn.gov/pdf/Franklin%20LUP%202%20SAPS%20TDR%20SH7%20Amended%20Feb%2022%202007.pdf, last visited June 14, 2009.

Gilbert, Arizona 2001. *General Plan, Chapter 10*, available at http://www. ci.gilbert.az.us/generalplan/chapter10.cfm#gateway, last visited June 22, 2009.

Maine State Planning Office 2004. *The Great American Neighborhood*, available at http://www.maine.gov/spo/landuse/docs/compplanning/guideto-livabledesign_greatamericanneighborhood2005.pdf., last visited June 9, 2009.

McHarris Planning & Design (n.d.). *Neighborhood Village Centers: Collier County, Florida* (on file with author.)

Mount Vernon, Washington. *Design Standards and Guidelines*, available at http://www.ci.mount-vernon.wa.us/imageuploads/Media-1003.pdf, last visited, June 30, 2009.

Plainfield, Illinois 2002. *Design Guidelines for Planned Unit Developments*, available at http://www.plainfield-il.org/departments/documents/PUDDesignGuidelines.pdf, last visited June 27, 2009.

Plainfield, Illinois 2005. *Residential Design and Planning Guidelines for Planned Unit Developments and Annexations*, available at http://www.plainfield-il.org/departments/documents/ResidentialDesignGuidelines.pdf, last visited June 29, 2009.

San Diego, California 1992. *North City Urbanizing Area Plan*, available at http://www.sandiego.gov/planning/community/profiles/ncfua/pdf/ncfuafullversion.pdf, last visited June 23, 2009.

Sarasota County, Florida. *Resource Management Area System Plan*, available at http://www.scgov.net/PlanningandDevelopment/CompPlan/documents/chap09_Sarasota2050.pdf, last visited August 6, 2009.

Scottsdale, Arizona 2001a. *General Plan 2001*, available at http://www.scottsdaleaz.gov/Assets/documents/generalplan/generalplan.pdf, last visited June 18, 2009.

Scottsdale, Arizona 2001b. *Sensitive Design Principles*, available at http://www.scottsdaleaz.gov/planning/general/sensitivedesign/designprin.asp, last visited June 23, 2009.

Scottsdale, Arizona Various Dates. *Architecture Design Guidelines*, available at http:// ww.scottsdaleaz.gov/planning/general/sensitivedesign/bldg-guidelns.asp, last visited June 18, 2009.

Sparks, Nevada 2004. *Design Standards Manual*, available at http://www.ci.sparks.nv.us/business/planning_dev/pdfs/SparksDSM2004TableofContent2004.pdf, last visited June 7, 2009.

Tucson, Arizona, Department of Urban Planning and Design 2005. *Houghton Area Master Plan*, available at http://www.tucsonaz.gov/planning/plans/all/hamp.pdf, last visited June 4, 2009.

U.S. Green Building Council. *LEED for Neighborhood Development Rating System, Proposed Ballot Draft*, available at http://www.usgbc.org/ShowFile. aspx?DocumentID=6146, last visited, October 30, 2009.

Vermont Planning Information Center 2007. *Vermont Land Use Planning Implementation Manual: Planned Unit Development*, available at http://www.vpic.info/pubs/implementation/pdfs/22-PUD.pdf, last visited July 23, 2009.

ORDINANCES

Clarion Associates 2004. *Tucson, Arizona Planned Community Development District*, Staff Review Draft (on file with author.)

Collier County, Florida (a). *Architectural and Site Design Standards*, available at http://www.colliergov.net/Index.aspx?page=897, last visited July 5, 2009.

Collier County, Florida (b). *Land Development Code*, available at http://www.municode.com/resources/gateway.asp?pid=13992&sid=9, last visited July 20, 2009.

Dearborn County, Indiana 2000. *Zoning Ordinance*, available at http://www.dearborncounty.org/planning/Official_Documents_files/Zoning%20Ordinance/ARTICLE%2016%20%20Planned%20Unit%20Development.pdf , last visited, June 28, 2009.

Durham, North Carolina. *Unified Development Ordinance*, available at http://www.durhamnc.gov/udo/mainPage.asp, last visited, July 3, 2009.

Fairfax County, Virginia. *Zoning Ordinance*, available at http://www.fairfax-county.gov/dpz/zoningordinance/articles/art06.pdf, last visited July 3, 2009.

Franklin, Tennessee 2008. *Zoning Ordinance*, available at http://www.franklintn.gov/pdf/Franklin%20Zoning%20Ordinance-%2011-11-08.pdf, last visited, June 24, 2009.

Greensboro, North Carolina. *Zoning Ordinance,* available at http://www.municode.com/resources/gateway.asp?sid=33&pid=10736, last visited, July 3, 2009.

Gunnison, Colorado. 2006. *Land Development Code*, available at http://www.codepublishing.com/CO/GUNNISON.HTML, last visited, June 28, 2009.

Lake County, Illinois. *Regulations for the Planned Development Residential, or "PDR" District*, available at http://www.co.lake.ca.us/Assets/CDD/ZoningOrd/Zoning+Article+13.pdf, last visited, July 9, 2009.

Orange County, Florida 2009. *West Horizon (Village) Development Code (Updates)*, available at http://www.orangecountyfl.net/NR/rdonlyres/

eat4nr3nqsk372jwve572sx2ubqujsyq2s5lcbsvgkgxn6mbzhant7zk-
catjcfemixvayuauxwek5tl3mrxsdkwkjw4e/UpdatestotheHorizonWest
VillageDevelopmentCodeOrdinanceRevisedDraft051309.pdf,
last visited, July 29, 2009.

Peoria, Arizona. *Zoning Ordnance*, available at http://www.peoriaaz.gov/upload-
edFiles/Peoriaaz/Departments/Community_Development/Planning_
and_Zoning/Zoning_Ordinances/14_22_PlannedUnitDevelopment.
pdf, last visited, June 28, 2009.

St. Joseph, Michigan 2007. *Zoning Ordinance*, available at http://www.sjcity.
com/pdfs/Zoning%20ordinance%20amended%20050409%20eff%20
051409.pdf., last visited June 28, 2009.

San Marcos, California. *Zoning Ordinance*, available at http://www.ci.san-
marcos.ca.us/Modules/ShowDocument.aspx?documentid=243, last visited July 5, 2009.

Santa Ana, California. *Planned Residential Development Ordinance*, available
at http://www.santa-ana.org/pba/planning/documents/PRD.pdf, last
visited, July 8, 2009.

Sarasota County, Florida. *Article 11. 2050 Regulations,* available at http://
www.municode.com/resources/gateway.asp?pid=11511&sid=9, last visited June 14. 2009.

Somerville, Massachusetts 1990. *Zoning Ordinance*, available at http://www.
ci.somerville.ma.us/CoS_Content/documents/Article%2016.pdf, last
visited July 8, 2009.

WEB SITES

American Planning Association
    planning.org
Congress for the New Urbanism
    cnu.org
Form Based Codes Institute
    formbasedcodes.org
National Association of Homebuilders
    nahb.org
SmartCode Central
    smartcodecentral.com
Urban Land Institute
    uli.org